# Open Heavens

# Open Heavens

## Meditations for Advent and Christmas

*Eugen Drewermann*

Translated by David J. Krieger

Edited by Joan Marie Laflamme and Bernd Marz

ORBIS BOOKS

Maryknoll, New York 10545

The Catholic Foreign Mission Society of America (Maryknoll) recruits and trains people for overseas missionary service. Through Orbis Books, Maryknoll aims to foster the international dialogue that is essential for mission. The books published, however, reflect the opinions of their authors and are not meant to represent the official position of the society.

English translation © 1991 Orbis Books, Maryknoll, New York 10545.
All rights reserved.
Manufactured in the United States of America.
Originally published in German by Patmos Verlag Düsseldorf.
Copyright © 1990 by Patmos Verlag.

**Library of Congress Cataloging-in-Publication Data**

Drewermann, Eugen.
    [Offene Himmel. English]
    Open heavens : meditations for Advent and Christmas / Eugen Drewermann; translated by David J. Krieger; edited by Joan Marie Laflamme and Bernd Marz.
        p.  cm.
    Translation of: Offene Himmel.
    ISBN 0-88344-775-4
    1. Advent—Meditations.  2. Christmas—Meditations.  3. Epiphany season—Meditations.  I. Laflamme, Joan Marie.  II. Marz, Bernd, 1953-    .  III. Title.
BX2170.A4D6513  1991
242'.33—dc20                                                    91-28323
                                                                    CIP

# Contents

Introduction to the English Edition      vii

## THE ADVENT SEASON

First Week of Advent      3

Second Week of Advent      27

Third Week of Advent      48

Fourth Week of Advent      73

## THE CHRISTMAS SEASON

Christmas      101

Second Day of Christmas      147

New Year      163

First Sunday after Christmas      176

Second Week after Christmas      181

Epiphany      193

After Epiphany      214

# Introduction to the English Edition

As we read the Christmas meditations and homilies of Eugen Drewermann, it quickly becomes clear that for him the Bible is not a mere quarry for propositions of faith, but a living voice calling us to conversion, radical change, and transformation. But the call to conversion is not an imposition from outside the human soul. Rather, it springs from within as a hope for the fulfillment of our deepest yearnings to be true to our inner self.

In Mary, the mother of Jesus, Drewermann finds a human face contemplating the mystery of God's birth in us. Joseph, the father of pragmatic trust, follows an unsettling dream. The stable in Bethlehem already contains within itself the cross of Golgotha. In their daring journey the astrologers become royalty. And each figure calls us to examine the meaning of the Christmas story for ourselves.

Such truths of Christianity, when grasped from within the human soul, as Drewermann bids us, are hardly "known" or "comprehended" as concepts. Rather, they embody a wisdom we appropriate as we journey through life. Eugen Drewermann, therapist, theologian, and pastor, helps us enter into the journey into ourselves even as we carry on the outer journey of everyday life.

The language of Father Drewermann is original and vital. He speaks out of and to the buried depths of the soul, out of and to the abysses within the human spirit. His words traverse the time spans of millennia, enter into the border regions of exotic cultures and religions, make us aware of the God who is never nearer than when apparently absent, the God who embraces the cosmos and reconciles transcendence and immanence. Poetic images find their real home and dramatic coalescence in God, the incomprehensible, the ground of all ground. And biblical narrative finds its continuation in our own present. Drewermann asks and answers two important questions: Where is Bethlehem? Where is the place where God can be born?

It is not merely a city fifteen miles south of Jerusalem, for the gospel of the birth of Jesus does not relate the beginning of his life; it really tells us of the beginning of our own lives as men and women, the story of our incarnation. Therefore, Bethlehem is wherever men and women are capable of suffering on account of inhumanity and wherever they hunger and thirst for the justice of God. Only in their hearts does God reside.

Just as the texts of the gospel compose events, narrate parables, describe actions in images, take up and vary motifs, so also are Drewermann's meditations a dynamic description of a way and not a static presentation of an unreachably high or pretentious goal.

What Jesus means to Drewermann is not that we objectively know the way the other person must go or even that we need to know it. The only thing we have to do is accompany the other person to that place where he or she wants to go in order to come home.

Such a theology of the way means setting off, stopping and resting, backtracking and taking detours, but it never implies a tiring longing and a deadly exhaustion. Jacob's struggle at Jabbok continues in every hour of this life if we learn to attend to the depth-dimension of "ordinary" events.

In these meditations Father Drewermann describes the way of the gospel. He retells what is well-known and discovers the new. That which here and there might appear repetitive discloses, in fact, a deeper meaning. New dimensions are opened up, habitual ways of thinking and experiencing are reversed and transposed, and undreamed of levels of reality are deciphered. Impression and expression mark both sides of one and the same reality, which falls together in God.

Drewermann has become a best-seller in Germany on three fronts. First, as a theological controversialist, he fearlessly raises trenchant criticism of the academic and ecclesiastical communities and their desiccated readings of Christian faith. Second, as a skilled interpreter of both scripture and fairy tales, he brings insights from depth-psychology to bear on how these stories illuminate the human situation. And third, as a pastor and liturgical celebrant, he weaves the talents of a skilled theologian and therapist into the rich tapestry of worship. These meditations represent the work of Bernd Marz, who brought together Father Drewermann's homilies; the doggedly accurate translation skills of David J. Krieger; and the efforts of Joan Marie Laflamme to render the book for an English-speaking audience.

# The
# Advent
# Season

# First Week
# of Advent

## The Son of Man Will Come

*"For as it was in the days of Noah, so it will be at the coming of the Son of Man. In [those] days before the flood, they were eating and drinking, marrying and giving in marriage, up to the day that Noah entered the ark. They did not know until the flood came and carried them all away. So will it be [also] at the coming of the Son of Man. Two men will be out in the field; one will be taken, and one will be left. Two women will be grinding at the mill; one will be taken, and one will be left.*

*Therefore, stay awake! For you do not know on which day your Lord will come. Be sure of this: if the master of the house had known the hour of the night when the thief was coming, he would have stayed awake and not let his house be broken into. So too, you also must be prepared, for at an hour you do not expect, the Son of Man will come"* (Mt 24:37-44).

When ultimate questions and defining moments, such as life and death, are at stake, we enter a nebulous, fearful twilight zone. Talking about God in these situations takes on the character of promise or threat. We share in the experience Jesus speaks of above.

It is beautiful to walk along the seashore, gazing over the water as it stretches toward the horizon. But when a low-pressure front intrudes and storm clouds threaten us, we become aware of something quite different. The wind howls over the embankment and the sea whips crowns of foam upon the beach. Who is able to look upon the sea without dread? One ducks for cover and leaves the raging ocean to the brave flight of the gulls.

To a person leading a certain kind of life, God is feared like a thief, like a shadowy, far-off danger. Among the saddest and most frightening words of Jesus are these about the coming of the Son of Man. Is it really a question of a distant future? Or are Jesus' experiences with his contemporaries finding expression in these disturbing words?

No matter how veiled the references to himself, Jesus still lets it be known that in his person exists all that one expects from salvation and all that one finds personified in the figure of the coming Son of Man. One needn't hope in a distant future or search for a utopia, for our calling as men and women lives in us and right next to us and can be heard in the words of Jesus. The endlessness of reality, the boundless beauty of the soul, and the enticing call of unlimited freedom are in the heart of every man and woman. So Jesus wanted to tell each one of us that we should have the courage to remember the dream of our lives. We should not think that salvation somehow comes from a distant place. What we long and hope for in life is our own being. Powerfully present in our most daring visions of ourselves is precisely the way of being God intends for us. We shouldn't deny or abandon our childhood dreams. Jesus beseeches each one of us to believe in his kingdom, to feel its truth and value, and thus to open our eyes to the beauty and greatness of each human being around us.

Jesus told us this in parables. His hands touched the eyes of people blind in sorrow, loneliness, and despair and raised them toward the light. Jesus touched the skin of people scarred by feelings of shame, impurity, and injury, and restored them to themselves — intact, whole, and fair to the eyes of all. How much Jesus believed in the beauty and worth of each human being! But with what bitterness he experienced the way we shut our ears, not wanting to hear; how we raise our hands before our eyes, not wanting to see; how we seal our lips, not wanting to speak. Why? Because a life constricted and trapped in the ghetto of fear always finds new threats and new reasons to defend itself, draws up barricades, and cuts itself off from salvation.

What can be done when people so identify themselves with what is not life and even anti-life that they begin to fear the coming of true existence with horror, experience the call of openness as torture, and perceive the message of God as an imposition? There is indeed dreadful despair, which no longer remembers the existence of hope; there is terrible resignation, which no longer knows what it means to dream; there is awful insanity, in which good and evil, virtue and vice, greatness and meanness no longer exist, but only monotony and confusion. This is nothingness inflated to a way of life. In the end one doesn't really live anymore; life is a chaotic vortex of accidents. Because of pure weakness and cowardice only circumstances remain, circumstances consecrated by the voice of irresponsibility—"I didn't know," "I hadn't heard," "I never saw," "I couldn't do anything." Only circumstances are blamed; they are the cause and the reason for everything. It is as if such persons hadn't felt the desire and claim of being called to lead their own life, to be individuals, to stand apart from the masses and the smoky veil of otherness. There are those who say we only begin to live and to exist as individuals when we separate ourselves from others. Certainly we belong with others, not just because we have been externally pushed into the same work, but because of the sameness of our nature, the sympathy of our hearts. But for this, we must first discover ourselves.

As Jesus learned, only those who have not completely lost the ability to suffer, who have not fully given up hope and the longing for another life, and who are still capable of shedding tears are ripe for salvation. These he beatified, for they were vulnerable enough to believe in another life and to find a meaningless existence unbearable. These are the people who yearn, perhaps unconsciously and unintentionally, but still with great passion, for the breakthrough—one can hardly speak of it otherwise—of salvation.

What Christ calls the "wakefulness for the breakthrough of God" belongs, depending upon how we see it, to the most wonderful or most terrible things that the human heart can contain. It is terrible when it breaks in like a deluge, like the biblical flood, tearing us away from everything. But it is wonderful when it is experienced as a courageous tenacity to the one hope, the one possibility.

This is a miracle that one sees again and again in people.

This is what Jesus repeatedly saw during his life. He saw how people who, like plants shrunk to thorny shapes after long years of spiritual draught and inner barrenness, suddenly flowered with the coming of rain. People can unexpectedly develop extraordinary powers and come to feel and know that now is the time upon which everything depends. They throw away their fear, break out of their prisons, and hold onto their life and nature. This is what Jesus wants to prepare us for. He wants to sensitize us to this moment, this chance that will suddenly come. We should never forget what we are called to be. And we should not call despair our happiness or try to drown our sadness in this world of inhumanity with the noisy commotion of false gaiety lest we suffer the same fate as those in Kierkegaard's story: A jester appears upon the stage of a theater and announces to the public that the theater is on fire. Everyone laughs and applauds. The jester disappears behind the curtain and appears once again. Very seriously he reports that the theater is burning. The audience applauds even more. And the balconies come crashing down amidst the rollicking laughter of all those who thought it was only a joke.

## The End of Time

*"Immediately after the tribulation of those days*

> *the sun will be darkened,*
>    *and the moon will not give its light,*
> *and the stars will fall from the sky,*
>    *and the powers of the heavens will be shaken.*

*And then the sign of the Son of Man will appear in heaven, and all the tribes of the earth will mourn, and they will see the Son of Man coming upon the clouds of heaven with power and great glory. And he will send out his angels with a trumpet blast, and they will gather his elect from the four winds, from one end of the heavens to the other.*

*"Learn a lesson from the fig tree. When its branch becomes tender and sprouts leaves, you know that summer is near. In the same way, when you see all these things, know that he is near, at the gates. Amen, I say to you, this generation will not pass away until all these things have taken place. Heaven and earth will pass away, but my words will not pass away. But of that day and hour no one knows, neither the angels of heaven, nor the Son, but the Father alone"* (Mt 24:29-36).

We almost always hear these words about the sudden coming of the end of time with feelings of terror and dread. These few places in the Bible that present the collapse of the heavens and the destruction of the world have been used, often and frighteningly, during times of fear and uncertainty. But I don't believe that the people who first heard these texts and wrote them down were themselves influenced by feelings of fear and horror. In the middle of the second century there was still a small group of Christians in Rome who expected the end of the world to come shortly. Just as the words of the gospel say: Before this generation has passed away, all these things will have taken place. They prayed that the kingdom of God would "quickly come," and they added "and may this world pass away," understanding that to be the correct interpretation of the entreaty in the Our Father.

How we conceive of the end of time is actually a question of how much we suffer under the present situation. The early church certainly suffered more from the world in which it lived than from any fear of that world's end. On the contrary. The course of the world, as it appeared to those who looked upon the death of Christ and the joy of his resurrection, was one sure road into the abyss.

These texts, with their talk of sun and moon and stars, present the end of the world essentially as a cosmic drama. Again and again visions of this sort were employed in Christianity in order to illustrate the end of the world in an external way, often giving concrete dates and times.

On this level there is little reason for concern. Our little planet still has a life span of several billion years. Even if the human race somehow manages to destroy itself and all life upon the earth, the history of the planet will continue. Our species came into being, even when one overestimates, only three or four million years ago, a mere fraction measured against the billions of years in which the history of the planet is reckoned. We describe historical dramas and catastrophes in centuries or at the most in millennia. For nature, this is an insignificant span.

In other words, these biblical texts are concerned not with the end of the planet earth or of the world in an external sense, but with all that can and should come to an end before we can begin a life that allows us to raise our eyes to the clouds of the heavens and realize the vision of humanity. Wherever we look, we block our own way and throw shadows upon our own hopes.

A world in which we invest our trust and expectations is a world in which there are no boundaries between us and our fellow human beings. How would our history appear freed from the narrow and confining borders drawn by national egoism and national security? The world that we yearn for must be a world in which men and women do not need to threaten each other with death in order to live together. How different the economic order of the world and the "security" of our political institutions would look if we could learn to do without the threats of war, without armaments, and without all the misery and fear that accompany them. The world we are hoping for—the only world in which a truly human life is possible—would be supported by the effort to understand one another and by an option to deal with every human need wherever we encounter it. How much of our normal way of life would we have to let go of, in order to gain in humanity?

We needn't fear that opening to another person would mean suppression and denial of our own personality. The flower that opens itself to the light does not deny itself; neither do we. The only question is, Where does a milder, warmer climate come from, a climate in which we can approach each other without defense, a climate in which we can believe in God and ourselves out of an abundance of trust?

Ever since the days of the early church we have believed that such a climate of trust, of warmth, of peace among all men and women has in principle already begun in the person of Jesus. Everything that he lived and said is so tangibly true that we need only do it ourselves. Still, whenever we try, we find reasons in the way the world is set up and in the way we interpret the world that stop us, block our good intentions, and impose against them a logic of contradiction and denial. In this sense a part of the world must always perish in order to make place for the kingdom of God. Wherever this occurs, we tear down stones from the prison of this world; freedom grows in our hearts and more of the light of God penetrates into the dungeon of our lives. The end of the world is not a terrible vision. It is the beginning of our true life.

In the images of the sun, the moon, and the stars, there still remain many ideals in which we believe, as we once believed in those heavenly bodies. Much must fall from the heaven of our values before we can more deeply understand God. So many of our trusted judgments and ideals are in reality false ideology and propaganda, unworthy of our confidence. But in our hearts we can often simply feel what is human. We don't need big words; we just have to do it. So simple and obvious is this that Jesus could say, When your left hand doesn't know what the right hand does, then that is true and right.

This world is simple when the rubbish falls away, and we can cross over a quaking earth with trust. May God be near us with his protection and his love. For in him we live and exist, always, until the end of time.

## Be Prepared

*"Immediately after the tribulation of those days*

> *the sun will be darkened,*
> *and the moon will not give its light,*
> *and the stars will fall from the sky,*
> *and the powers of the heavens will be shaken.*

*And then the sign of the Son of Man will appear in heaven.*
*"But of that day and hour no one knows, neither the angels*
*of heaven, nor the Son, but the Father alone. . . . Therefore,*
*stay awake! For you do not know on which day your Lord*
*will come. Be sure of this: if the master of the house had*
*known the hour of the night when the thief was coming, he*
*would have stayed awake and not let his house be broken*
*into. So too, you also must be prepared, for at an hour you*
*do not expect, the Son of Man will come" (Mt 24:29-30, 36,*
*42-44).*

At the beginning of the new liturgical year, the beginning of
Advent, we wish each other the grace and peace of the promised
coming of the Son of Man. But the terrifying vision of the
destruction of the world breaks into the calm of such wishing
and hoping. Why, we ask of these apocalyptic visions, does the
beginning of the new, of that which saves, have to be purchased
at the price of the terrible destruction of everything that exists?

There is much in this text that we can only understand by
reflecting on biblical conditions during the first century. The
early church interpreted the leveling of Jerusalem under the
assault of the Roman cohorts as a sign of the end not only of
the Jewish people, but of the entire world. A radical change of
all things seemed imminent. They heard an echo of the thinking
of the prophet Jeremiah from six hundred years before. Jeremiah, the son of a priest from southern Jerusalem, was devoted
and faithful to the Temple and to the tradition of his fathers.
Yet he came to the conclusion that the priests in the Temple

were lying and the prophets of the court perjuring themselves. Jeremiah believed that the Temple in Jerusalem and the walls of the holy city would have to be trampled down and ground to dust by the enemies of God before God could begin again from the beginning. And Jeremiah believed that God would no longer write upon tables of stone, but upon the hearts of men and women.

In the days of Jesus, apocalyptic groups believed with an almost mathematical certainty and an inner peace that they could see such an event coming again. Such thinking reflects a bizarre kind of hope that grows out of extreme suffering on account of existing conditions. One almost wishes for the end of the painful status quo as soon as possible, and the more terrible and quicker that end, the better.

Under certain conditions, it is possible to look at the entire world in this way, to see in it a condition that almost deserves to be done away with as quickly and as thoroughly as possible. The statistics speak for themselves, and they send a strange message. Indeed, the headlines have been the same for over a decade: increasing $CO_2$, the ozone gap, the destruction of the tropical forests, the encroaching desert, over-population, hunger and poverty, the dangers of atomic energy. Everything seems to be coming together. A catastrophe in the next fifty years or so seems unavoidable. But as this text says quite simply, despite apocalyptical calculations we don't know the day and the hour. Astronomers may predict that sometime in four and a half or five and a half million years the sun will lose its light. Perhaps one day geneticists will tell us that they have calculated when the human race must inevitably die out. But such prognoses don't help us to live today; we need a little bit of hope in order to realize our humanness, and now this text begins to speak in a quite different way within us. Just when we think that the catastrophe is upon us and we see it coming near, what appears to us? Not the darkness, hopelessness, and the abyss that the text describes, but rather, the sign of the Son of Man will be written upon the heavens and in the clouds like a torch.

The standard for everything, in destruction as in construction, is our humanness. We can examine the feelings that arise when, because of a breakthrough to a greater maturity, a more generous attitude, a broader, more human self-realization, the old order that we had learned breaks apart and falls away. How much it costs us to leave a world whose inhumanity we know well! From time to time we experience small apocalypses of this sort. We might want to believe they are less serious than the cosmic apocalypses. But to say it pointedly, I don't know a single person who despairs upon hearing that fifty million men, women, and children are starving in the southern hemisphere. To take our life on account of that would, paradoxically, be considered crazy. But people really can despair when a loved one dies, or when an accident occurs right next to them. It's as though our feelings are only capable of intensity within a circle of about ten people. Our entire emotional economy is set up by nature for a small group; beyond that events become more and more abstract.

It can be, however, that it is precisely in our nearest circle and in dealing with ourselves that we have learned forms of cruelty that become all the more unbearable the more we take them for granted. Take, for example, a woman who as a child learned that she had been born into a world that had no use for her. No one is really guilty for this. It just happens. Perhaps her father was totally occupied with building up a business. He needed the money for his family. He was conscious of his duty and loyal to his family. And perhaps his wife helped as much as she could with the business, giving it all her energy. In this situation the birth of a child can be a minor catastrophe. Despite much love and responsibility, at this point of time it really shouldn't have happened. The father and mother don't admit this to themselves or to their child, at least as long as they have good intentions. But the child very soon feels the truth, even after only a few weeks, and this feeling becomes fixed and hardens. Suppose that such a child tries to do everything she can to lessen the burden upon her parents. She tries to be as thoughtful, attentive, sensitive, obliging, helpful, accommodating, and uncomplaining as possible. Later, when she herself marries and has children, she will do everything in order to save her children from a similar fate. She will become all the more dutiful, helpful, devoted, and attentive. We can assume that this task will become too great a burden for her and, precisely because she is overburdened and internally upset, her child is also finally unwanted, and again she doesn't tell her this. The child has the duty to be happy in order to pay back the mother for having meant so well. And there arises a terror of caring which ends after fifteen or eighteen years when the scales fall from the mother's eyes. Her daughter is a drug addict, or she rushes into a bad relationship, or she fails in her career, and the mother, now forty years old, must face the fact that, despite all her good intentions and such great effort, she has done harm.

The more we talk to people, the clearer their lacks appear — and the clearer we see how difficult life can be. A woman like this must learn that she also has a right to exist. She has to take for herself what she never was allowed to have. She must spend time on her own interests and win back a little bit of humanness for herself.

It should be clear that this license lets everything melt away that until then had been duty and order. And this collapse is like a breakdown of everything. Then the sun, moon, and stars fall from the sky; then the world of father, mother, and all the highly esteemed ideals lose the power to illuminate, and she becomes disenchanted; then the earth quakes beneath her feet, everything whirls around her head; then everything seems sheer madness. Nevertheless, this breakdown is a time of a new maturity, so that the gospel can say with incredible joy, When all this has passed, then it will be as in springtime when buds shoot forth. When the frozen landscape thaws and the apparently tidy world is transformed into mud and mire and flooding streams, we can only pass through with dirty feet. Only by the breakdown of a clear and frozen world does life return.

Against all those who make calculations about the apocalypse, Jesus says, You cannot determine in advance the day of the real transformation, of the coming of final and decisive humanness; no one knows it. And how do we live with the frightening possibility that it could occur any minute? Jesus says, Not even the angels in heaven know what God will do. There are very few places in the Christian Scriptures where Jesus calls himself the Son of God. Paradoxically, this text is one of them. He continues, Not even the Son knows the hour.

Jesus, trusting fully in the Father, is clearly in agreement with this blessed uncertainty. This grants us the courage to live *today*, and to live as well as possible. If we had even the slightest idea of what would happen to us in, say, two and a half years or in twenty-five years—how we would die or, worse, what mistakes we would make, what our destiny would be—how would we find the courage to go through the wall of darkness toward the rising sun? It is a gift of nature that, despite all our reason, we finally must learn to be at peace, the way animals naturally are, by means of faith. Animals are full of fear at the moment when death attacks them, but Nature itself spares them constant fear and the feeling of being hunted. We don't know what will come. And that which, because of uncertainty, makes us afraid, we overcome through faith. To exist *today*—that is the beginning of Advent. Care not for tomorrow! Only in this way is the future prepared for; only thus do we learn to practice humanness and not to calculate and reckon. I think it is a great mistake when we always try to plan the future, when we are always concerned to act in such a way that things turn out for the best. We lose sight thereby of the fact that there may be something more important than responsibly acting for the preservation of a future generation. More important than *right acting* is *really existing*. False ideals must dissolve, and then we will see before us the image of the Son of Man. There are clear feelings within us of what we really are and of what really concerns us. To act accordingly, without delay, brings us and those around us nearer to God. At the end of fear stands the peace of trusting.

It is said that when someone asked Martin Luther what he would do if he knew he must die that very afternoon, he answered that he would go into his garden and plant a tree. When asked a similar question, St. Francis de Sales said he would think some more about what a white knight in a chess game would do on E8. It is holy carelessness to live the present day to the fullest, for tomorrow is God's, and thus ours too.

# May the Lord Not Find You Sleeping

*"Be watchful! Be alert! You do not know when the time will come. It is like a man traveling abroad. He leaves home and places his servants in charge, each with his work, and orders the gatekeeper to be on the watch. Watch, therefore; you do not know when the lord of the house is coming, whether in the evening, or at midnight, or at cockcrow, or in the morning. May he not come suddenly and find you sleeping. What I say to you, I say to all: 'Watch!' " (Mk 13:33-37).*

The words of this text are the last words of the Lord immediately before his passion. It is the summary of everything he has to say, and it is the reason he must suffer. The first words of Mark's gospel were a promise and a command: The kingdom of God is close at hand, convert. His last words are that no stone will remain upon another, for everything will be turned upside-down. God will not let himself be stopped by the defiance of men and women. But why will salvation be based upon so much overturning, instead of on conversion, as Jesus himself had hoped?

Jesus carried a bright image of humanity in his heart. He himself was so near to God that he wanted to bring every human being into such closeness to God. His way of seeing people was so open, so free, so much sustained by affection, sympathy, and warmth that he wanted to believe of all people, and make all people believe, that they had the chance to realize God in their hearts without delay and without hesitation. If only men and women would understand the greatness to which they are called, the value they carry within themselves, how much respect they owe one another, then a kingdom of freedom, peace, and understanding could immediately arise in this world.

Some theologians, in view of the fate of Jesus, say that his prophecies about the coming of the kingdom of God were mistaken. The kingdom of God has not come; rather, the church has come in its place. Two thousand years of world history have passed without the coming of the kingdom of God. Many kingdoms have been founded upon this earth and have written their names into history with blood and violence, but the kingdom of God is farther away than ever. Jesus made this mistake, they say, because of his love for humanity, his presumptuous divine vision of human beings.

But are we really allowed to lie to ourselves and to calm ourselves in this way? Are we to call the Lord a fool and a dreamer, even when we have theological permission and are guided by an enlightened view of history? Or must we not say now, at the very gates of Advent, that Jesus' dream of humanity was absolutely right, that he spoke the truth when he said that every man and woman was immediately present to God and that the feeling of fear of each other would disappear in the trust we have in God?

There are, in fact, people — and at the time of Jesus they were almost omnipotent — for whom it is always too early to speak of God. For them, it is never time to be serious about humanity; it is too early and untimely to be serious about God upon the plowed-up and blood-soaked face of this earth. They consider it an error to grant God a central place in human life. For them, God always comes too soon; there is never a right time. Things have always been as they are now; therefore, they should never change. We have learned how to live in this world, and so we don't need to learn anything new. We have our established customs and habits, and therefore it is bothersome when something new comes up. We have our peace and quiet, we know how to get along, and therefore we don't need the tumult of new ideas, prophecies, and solutions. If such lethargy is right, Jesus is wrong. If laziness and listlessness of heart are right, then Jesus is indeed a fool. But his last words to us, before he was crushed by the boots of history, were, Stay awake!

These are words that the early church understood in an apocalyptic sense. The church said to herself that if Jesus had to perish on account of this world, then it must mean that this world must be destroyed before the truth can come. And is it so wrong for the church to have thought this? The world we think we know so well is founded upon iron pillars that Jesus wanted to shake. And we are much too caught up in the fog of custom and habit to dare to take the point of view of the gospel seriously. Jesus questions, in his time as well as today, whether the world as it is is human.

One of the iron pillars of our lethargy, which Jesus wanted to shake, was our acceptance of the fact that human relationships are corrupted by mere money. Our entire society is based upon money. The administration of our society in the form of politics is based upon money. Most human relationships are based upon money. No, please don't contradict me. We in the West believe in God and have been Christians for fifteen hundred years, more or less. So then explain to me how it is possible that whenever we come into contact with another culture, it learns not about God but about crass materialism. The people learn that there is no value, religious, human, or natural, except money. Obviously the only "truth" we export is our knowledge of how to destroy nature and humanity and abuse God in the name of money. We cannot destroy God, but we can and do defame and ideologize him.

The other pillar to which we cling is security based upon power. We are prepared to offer everything to this ideology, this idol. The world is reeling drunkenly toward the abyss, but we consider it perfectly normal and unavoidable to make ourselves secure by terrifying and threatening others. We call it freedom, self-defense, responsibility, and political prudence. For the sake of our own security, we have acquired the ability, each of us, to blow up, gas, and contaminate everything and everyone on this earth I don't know how many times over. Nothing satisfies our need to be secure. We stockpile supplies to excess, we spread deadly poverty, and we take it all for granted with the excuse that the kingdom of God *can't* come, it's not yet time. We should just go on living as we have always lived; it has always been right and good and, therefore, it will be all right tomorrow. And he who says this is a self-made apocalypse, that this world, if one goes on like this, will go directly to destruction, is a fool, a dreamer, a troublemaker, a madman, certainly someone without any knowledge of politics. The only question is how to get rid of him as quickly as possible.

At the beginning of his preaching Jesus said that God was near to those who hunger and thirst, who suffer, who yearn for something more, who are not established and satisfied with the status quo, who have the courage to expect something heretofore undreamed of. He said that God was near to those who cry out in despair and come to know a hope beyond the existing situation, who long for another world because they already carry it within their hearts, because they need it in order to be truly human, because they need it in order to live. This is obviously what Jesus wanted to say with his last words before the passion. He wanted the dissatisfaction, receptiveness, sensitivity, and vigor to expect something new. He wanted the courage to comprehend that the old was finished, the uncompromising attitude necessary to throw away the past like a worn-out coat. He wanted the boldness to look forward through the darkness and to believe more in the stars than in the night. May the Son of Man come at midnight, for despair will bring him into the world. And may he come late in the evening, when tiredness will await him. May he come when the cock crows, for then the dawn will await him. Oh, that he may come! May a new world come! These were the prayers of the early church. It was with these prayers that the early church celebrated the eucharist. May this world pass away; thy kingdom come!

We need to carry this attitude over into our private lives. Wherever we encounter each other we need to be like an alert gardener of the soul, who makes sure that each new sprout of hope does not die, but is strengthened, who watches over each stirring of the imagination, each awakening of new courage, every trace of freedom, every resolve to think for oneself, every strength with which we grasp more firmly our own being, every bud of unselfishness and generosity in dealing with one another. Every attempt to break out of the shadows of fear deserves to be sheltered and protected, cared for and guarded, and in the depths of the heart, accepted, blessed, and welcomed. Christ said that what he says to us, he says to all, Stay awake! He means, Stop trying to calm and reassure yourselves! The world is not in order as it is, and the way we have been taught to live is probably not the right way. We need to change all this. We must accept disquietude in order to come to know peace. We have to dare to change things radically in order to become at one with ourselves. We need to learn, to accept, and to accomplish the ruin of much that was said to be holy before we will be able to feel God more deeply in our hearts, worship him in gratitude, encounter him more humbly, and believe in him more humanly.

When the Son of Man comes, Christ said, it will be like a man who has left his house, but upon his return does not want to find it misused, devastated, transformed into chaos; he wants to find all men and women just as God created them, unblemished, united, and at peace. May this world perish — this world of devastation, fear, laziness, lethargy, lack of imagination, greedy interests, legitimation by means of a thousand lies. May the kingdom of peace come — the kingdom of truth, mercy, courage, individual maturity, and value for each and every person, the kingdom of happiness for every human being who sees the light of this world. Let us watch over every seed of hope.

## Eternity Is Waiting for Us

*"There will be signs in the sun, the moon, and the stars, and
on earth nations will be in dismay, perplexed by the roaring
of the sea and the waves. People will die of fright in anticipation of what is coming upon the world, for the powers of
the heavens will be shaken. And then they will see the Son of
Man coming in a cloud with power and great glory. But when
these signs begin to happen, stand erect and raise your heads
because your redemption is at hand." . . .*

*"Beware that your hearts do not become drowsy from
carousing and drunkenness and the anxieties of daily life, and
that day catch you by surprise like a trap. For that day will
assault everyone who lives on the face of the earth. Be vigilant
at all times and pray that you have the strength to escape the
tribulations that are imminent and to stand before the Son of
Man" (Lk 21:25-28, 34-36).*

What may we hope for, and what may we expect?

There are the official optimists who confidently hope that the
world can become better and better. For them the possibility of
failure, tragedy, or collapse is unthinkable. When someone
speaks of such things they call that person a cynic, a pessimist,
a defeatist, or simply a hopeless character. In the eyes of such
optimists Christians are incorrigible millennialists, completely
disillusioned about the course of human history and the world.
It is true that, as at Golgotha, the very logic of human history —
not merely an unhappy accident or a minor disturbance, but its
central theme — has been to persecute, slander, and destroy love
as soon as it appears. It is clear that the entire logic of power
and violence will desecrate and trample down freedom. One can
only hope with all one's heart that this kind of history will come
to an end as quickly as possible.

But what is human history if not the administration of ego-
tistical interests in little things as well as in big ones? We open
the newspaper and read that we can expect Christmas sales of
over ten million dollars. Consumption is rising and if consump-

tion rises we are doing the right thing; we are contributing to the expansion of the market, the growth of investments, economic progress, reduction of unemployment. This is good news indeed. It has its economic reason and its own logic. But again, a traitor to the nation's prosperity might say that this sort of good news at the cost of millions of starving people every year should come to an end as soon as possible. Christianity consists in seeing historical "reason" as one big nightmare of inhumanity.

We are told that development is only possible when progress pays off—materially, of course. Let's say it openly, those who are capable and efficient have to be rewarded, paid off, transformed into salaried slaves. But what if Christianity is right? What if it is possible, God knows how, to be concerned with something other than the obscene pocketbook, to have hopes and visions of humanity that go far beyond managed egoism? And what if we are destroying ourselves when we continue in the same old ways, feeling secure with idle hearts, thoughtlessness, and self-satisfaction? This alone, that things go on as before, is already the end. Nothing needs to change. We don't need a spectacle; signs in the sun, moon, and stars are thoroughly superfluous. There is no light shining above us, neither by day nor by night; there are no stars we can follow, barefooted, longing for something more, as if we were possessed by hope in the darkness. The fact is that the earth and its peoples are filled with fear, that the sea and the abyss are close at hand— already we hear the roaring.

When someone talks like this, he or she makes everyone afraid and causes them to plug their ears. "It's always been so, it will probably continue to be so. . . ." But Christianity knows that it doesn't pay to be afraid of catastrophes, certainly not of those that can only purify. It doesn't pay to fear destruction that leads to a more true form of human existence. How much of what is deadly in us, of the totally banal and routine, must pass away before we can really begin to live? How much freedom from merely apparent security, phoney seductions, from the corruption of all values and ideals do we need before we can trust ourselves to lead a life worthy of the name?

The early Christians couldn't see things any other way. It was possible to kill Jesus, but not the life that he wanted to bring.

If anything in this world is true, it is the words of the Sermon on the Mount: blessed are the poor in spirit, blessed those who weep, blessed those who can still mourn, that is, mourn for this — one often would like to say, damned — earth. They will have hope. They are not the living dead. They are not yet buried. Watch over yourselves, Jesus says in his last great vision in the gospel of Luke, be careful of intoxication, drunkenness, and the worries of the day. We can live in this way. We can conform, when we want, so that we are part of the crowd, doing as everyone does, living life as a party or holiday, or as sleep-walkers, or like moles, blindly burrowing in the dark.

We human beings can't bear this way of dying, and it isn't right for us either. In front of us lies the open space of eternity, and this earthly life, the few decades that we spend here, does not need to be and should not become a living trap in which we are constantly standing under the scythe of death, the past, and the already settled nothingness of everything. We can hope beyond the end. Much must pass away before we can rise from the dead, and not even death can terrify us. Eternity is waiting for us.

The hope in this vision is that what is valid in little things can be extended to the entire world. This planet, our solar system, our galaxy with its hundred billion fixed stars, even the hundred billion galaxies will cease to exist. Everything will pass, the sun in five billion years, the cosmos in fifty billion years — all this will sooner or later be calculated with certainty.

But what about our lives, and what about God? What about the destiny of the human race? We have to answer these questions, and the answer is always the same. We have the right to dare to love in the face of fear. We have the possibility to broaden our hearts against narrowness and suffocation. We have reason to hope beyond the grave, beyond death, beyond the destruction of everything. When the curtain is torn aside, our eyes will see the light.

## The Kingdom Is in Our Hands

*"People will die of fright in anticipation of what is coming upon the world, for the powers of the heavens will be shaken. And then they will see the Son of Man coming in a cloud with power and great glory. But when these signs begin to happen, stand erect and raise your heads because your redemption is at hand."* . . .

*"When you see these things happening, know that the kingdom of God is near."* . . .

*"Beware that your hearts do not become drowsy from carousing and drunkenness and the anxieties of daily life, and that day catch you by surprise like a trap" (Lk 21:26-28, 31, 34).*

One can hardly proclaim the coming of Jesus as the Son of Man in a more contradictory way. We prepare ourselves for a time of stillness, meditation, and peace, and then it is ushered in with the bombastic fanfare of images of the destruction of the world and the breakdown of everything. We ask ourselves, Why? Cannot peace be attained gently from within as a gift without these terrible pictures of destruction? But entire passages from the Christian Scriptures testify that this is not so, that between our incarnation and that which we call history lies a deep chasm, a collapse of everything, an end of the status quo, and a completely new beginning.

As long as life is more or less good to us and we can stand calmly upon this earth, images of the destruction of the world, as in this gospel, shock, worry, and disturb us. But there are moments when we experience ourselves and the world around us with so much pain that we hope it will all come to an end as quickly as possible. People who can no longer stand this world, who experience life as torture to the point of madness, are peculiarly calmed when they hear that this world—one has to say it, thank God—will not last forever. For example, in 1945 the German people invisibly separated into two groups. There were the people who heard the news from the eastern front and were suddenly horrified. Despite the lofty words on the radio, they suddenly knew and felt what was happening and that the catastrophe was inexorably closing in. But there were others who had secretly wished for a long time that the Third Reich would collapse as quickly as possible. For these people the same news was the beginning of hope. It is possible for us to long for calamity when the present situation is revolting, inhuman, and wholly unbearable.

So what can Christians contribute here? The writers of the apocalyptic visions in the Christian Scriptures thought there was something to be learned from the life of Jesus of Nazareth for the entire world and for all time. And that is, If it is possible systematically and consequently to crush the best, most courageous, most wonderful human being who ever lived among us, and to do so only a short time after he publicly appeared, just a couple of months perhaps, or after two years at the most; and if it is possible to do so not because he made some error in judgment or failed in some duty, but simply because the iron laws and precisely functioning mechanism of our entirely normal system of justice, our history, our morality *had* to destroy him, then everything we think we know and hold as normal is nothing but a single barbaric lie, and *nothing* we have been taught to believe in is true.

Either — or.

Either the dream of Jesus of Nazareth of the kingdom of God upon earth is a fantastic, anarchic, completely crazy dream, that one must oppose, because it causes men and women to hope beyond all measure, because it incites people to utopian ideas, because it claims that it is possible for men and women to live in freedom and personal dignity and says that they do not need to constantly bow to the harassment of those in power. If this dream of Jesus of Nazareth were dangerous, then his execution is the refutation of all these fantasies that he intended to bring into the world. We can calm ourselves, for we took care of the matter quickly. The death on the cross is the best refutation, and the world can relax again. Each one will return to his or her daily work with the patience of an animal, a horse, an ass, or an ox, and nothing will have changed.

Or the dream of Jesus of Nazareth is completely true. It

didn't fit into his time, and it doesn't fit into our time. But each one of us can know that it is true, for it touches us in the depths of our being. It reverberates with truth and a longing within; we can *feel* that the kingdom of God is near. If this is so, then his death is the uncovering of all the forces in us that oppose goodness, freedom, and humanness. His death on Good Friday is the apocalypse, the revelation of an inhumanity to which we have become so accustomed that we hardly even notice it anymore.

It is enough to give a couple of small examples. This dreamer from Nazareth imagined he could teach people that if someone strikes you on the one cheek, then you should present the other cheek as well. He thought he could satisfy all men and women with this teaching. He thought we could free ourselves from the senseless mechanism of reaction and counter-reaction, of blow and counter-blow, and learn a small bit of fearless sovereignty. It appears that he never really knew this world. Don't we have to say to him: My dear man, you're wasting your time with human beings. You imagine we can do things that are impossible for us. Even two thousand years after your death our civil order, the laws themselves, specify that eighteen-year-olds can be taught to kill other human beings in the most efficient way and with the most modern technology. This may even be a duty. Soldiers are forced to swear under oath that they will do everything necessary to defend their people and their nation. History teaches that to be free means to have teeth like a wolf and to be able to bite anyone who is suspected of being an enemy. Security, stability, and historical reason demand it. But such logic can only be maintained at the price of truth; pure goodness refutes it at every turn. That man from Nazareth stirs people up when he tells them that peace is easily attained and near at hand. He subverts the order of things we know so well.

The same applies when Jesus says that we don't need possessions and wealth, that as human beings we are so great and rich and beautiful that we don't need to show off our belongings like the peacock displays its tail feathers, that we can meet each other in truth and become dear to one another in love. *That* is a dream! *That* is a dream! That man knows nothing about money, about the circulation of goods, about business. He understands nothing at all about the normal assurances of civilized life. He has no knowledge of reality, or so it appears. How loudly we shout that it isn't going to work. How we find a thousand reasons to silence the man from Nazareth.

One has to suffer a lot because of this world in order to understand Jesus when he says that those who weep and mourn are blessed by God, for they don't want this world anymore. They think their dreams are more real than our contemptible materialism and militarism and all the rest. These people hope that the sun and moon and all the stars will fall from the sky. Everything in which we think we see our sublime and lofty ideals of power and glory and greatness, everything that we believe to be high and noble in the heaven of our ideals, as high as the stars above us, the guidelines according to which we lead our lives—everything will have to pass away, because it isn't true, because our entire heaven of ideals is a lie. And we will be afraid of the roaring of the sea, of all that wells up from the underground of emotion and passion when we don't watch out. And the earth will begin to shake. Only when human beings can't bear this world any longer will they say to themselves, Thank God that it has come. Only with a new beginning can we start to become truly human. This is what the string of apocalyptic visions means. They tell us that when everything upon which we thought we could depend disintegrates, then we need not despair. Rather, we can stand up, for we carry before us the image of true humanity. In symbolic language we hear that the Son of Man will come upon the clouds of heaven and that we will then finally be able to see that to which God has called us.

Of course, it can also happen that, out of sadness instead of hope, we resign ourselves, that we drown our pain in drunkenness, that we succumb to our everyday worries and just go on as always, giving up the need for humanness and burying the hope for truth. This numbing spell helps us to pretend that this world is not a trap in which fear holds us captive and from which we cannot escape. But it is possible to remain aware of the pain, for it teaches us hope. It is possible to preserve a feeling of suffering, for it exercises us in joy. It is possible to agree with the man from Nazareth, who spoke words upon the shore of Lake Gennesareth that changed everything till the end of the world, till the coming of the Son of Man. An Advent of upheaval, an Advent of a new beginning; Jesus says we have it in our hands.

# Second Week
# of Advent

## Asking the Questions That Matter

*John wore clothing made of camel's hair and had a leather belt around his waist. His food was locusts and wild honey. At that time Jerusalem, all Judea, and the whole region around the Jordan were going out to him and were being baptized by him in the Jordan River as they acknowledged their sins. . . .*

*"I am baptizing you with water, for repentance, but the one who is coming after me is mightier than I. I am not worthy to carry his sandals. He will baptize you with the holy Spirit and fire. His winnowing fan is in his hand. He will clear his threshing floor and gather his wheat into his barn, but the chaff he will burn with unquenchable fire" (Mt 3:4-6, 11-12).*

No figure in the Bible allows us to see the greatness and limits of a prophet so clearly as John the Baptist. He is a man between two ages, a man at an earth-shaking moment.

How is he described? He is clothed in camel's hair, wearing a belt of leather, emaciated like the plants of the desert and eating whatever comes to hand from the crevasses between the rocks. At the time I studied theology, I was taught that it was typical for the prophets of the Hebrew Scriptures to want to return to the time when Israel wandered about in the desert, led by the strong arm of God, fearing him, looking day and night in hope to the column of fire and smoke, knowing no other shield than God, with awe in their hearts for no other God than their own. The prophets, I was taught, despised the cultured way of life of agrarian society with its distractions, sensuality, unnatural

27

confusion, its sloth, and its inability to hear God. Or, if God *was* heard, he was not obeyed. John was the youngest, the last, and the best of this line of desert prophets. None of my teachers of theology ever told me what today we all know; namely, that these men who proclaimed an alternative were perhaps called by God—with their radicality, with their shrill words, with their trumpeting of the last judgment—to save life from its threatening doom.

What if the picturesque and grotesque costume of this man on the banks of the Jordan is taken literally? What if the entire road into what we call culture, or worse still, civilization, turns out to be an error, a long trek into inhumanity? What if those people we have driven onto reservations and to the margins of society are much more similar and closer to John the Baptist than we suppose? Some of the sayings of their wise men and women—words from people who live in tepees, who love the plains and the steppes—have been preserved. They speak about what we call normal life, and about humanity and piety, with cutting discernment, penetrating comprehension, and irrefutable clarity. If we wanted to translate, and I mean carefully translate, the preaching of John the Baptist into their way of thinking, it wouldn't necessarily sound like a vision of the end of the world. It would be more like a question, a provocation. And then one would have to answer an entire kaleidoscope of questions in terms of how reality is seen and perceived through the senses.

We would find ourselves being asked, How can you people see God with your eyes? Everything you see is distorted by greed and craving. You look at nothing on earth for the pure pleasure of it; you want to possess whatever you see. You can't just look at a tree and let it stand; you have to ask how much it would bring if it were cut down. You cannot simply enjoy a river; you have to ask how much money you could make if you owned it, how much energy it produces, how much it could produce if it were dammed. Thus also with the mountains, the plains, the oceans. You can't even look at the stars without wondering what sort of atomic fire you could make in order best to destroy yourselves. You can't look into space without thinking about how to transform the reaches of the cosmos into a field of battle full of

armaments, of machines of destruction, of powers of annihila-
tion. Whatever you see is stamped with greed, with devastation,
and with covetousness. And look at yourselves! Between you
there is only avarice. Who belongs to whom? Who can dominate
whom? Who can control whom? Who can rape and exploit
whom? How can you see God with such eyes? How can you even
see each other with such eyes?

And take your ears. How can you hear God if you unceasingly
fill your ears with bawling, noise, commotion, and inanities?
With the push of a button you could listen to the most beautiful
music, to Mozart, Beethoven, Tchaikovsky; you could hear the
best interpretations of Schiller or Goethe, but instead you run
around all day till your nerves tremble, till your ears ring. You
listen to words that are nothing more than bluster, babel, and
bedlam. This you call normal. It would be better if you heard
nothing at all! But please, no real ideas; they are too bothersome. Please, no deep reflection; it's too unsettling. Please, no
meditation; it brings you too close to yourselves. No, better to
deaden the ears, better the dullness, the din, the dumbness,
better to sit with both hands covering the organs that were made
to hear what others are saying, to help communicate ideas. How
can you hear God when living amid such clamor? And how can
you understand other people, when you make yourselves dumb?

And take your mouths. Most of your speech is vulgar. You
immediately strike out at others: "I'm right and you're wrong,"
"I know, and you have to listen." Commands, threats, orders,
self-righteousness, outbreaks of anger and revenge—these issue
from your mouth. Or you gossip about others. You draw each
through the mud and the filth; you spit venom at one another.
Do you think God can find a place in your mouths?

And your hands are the worst of all. Whatever they touch,
they make dirty; whatever they grab, they destroy. Where you
have passed by, the world is transformed into a wasteland.
Before you came, it was in flower.

Just a couple of yards further and the abyss will swallow us.
No one today, I believe, really doubts this. Our system of injustice, sadism, and violence is filled with deceit, inhumanity, self-
incurred ignorance, and hypocrisy. It cannot last long.

I could transpose all this into the style of John the Baptist and then every word would be like a whiplash, every sentence a terrible cry, every phrase like rolling thunder. And my mouth and hands are eager to attempt this. But it would take a hundred John the Baptists to spread the word around the world that this is the way it is. Let him come, we wish to ourselves! He is right!

This is the greatness of a prophet. His limits are just as clear. What does the fear the prophets incite really accomplish? What do the visions of the end of the world bring? What happens when one teaches people to see and to fear? Fear is good in the animal kingdom; it sharpens the senses and facilitates escape. By jumping away, an animal is saved from danger. Contrariwise, most human mistakes are made because we are afraid. We are the only creatures who can so twist fear that finally everything can be distorted. This is the limitation for the prophets; because they are right about everything, finally everything goes wrong, that is, if we listen to them *alone*.

The one who came after the Baptist was not as his predecessor described him, "His winnowing fan is in his hand; he will clear his threshing floor and gather his wheat into his barn; but the chaff he will burn in a fire that will never go out." Jesus never thought like this, he never felt these things, he never acted like this. What he wants is precisely the opposite. How to open hands that are cramped into fists? How to make our hands so rich that they are able to share? How to caress the hand so that it becomes tender and able to give life? How to touch the hand so that it becomes pure and so that everything that it handles is made beautiful? *These* are Jesus' questions.

How to talk in such a way that ears are opened and souls moved by words of truth? How to speak with such friendliness that fear vanishes from the heart and that person opens to his or her own life? How to form human words such that the voice sings and the human heart becomes an instrument that plays and embodies this melody? *These* are Jesus' questions.

How to make the mouth able to speak in such a way that friendliness and trust come forth? How to speak strong words that appeal to the heart and bring about peace, freedom, and justice, not imperiously demand them? How is it possible to form the mouth so that the words it speaks are as soft and close and as loving as a caress of the lips?

And how to open the eyes so that they mirror the stars and shine with the discovery of happiness? How to put the radiance of eternity and a trust in the goodness of the world into the eyes? How to make people see the beauty of all things and be thankful for the beauty of their own being? *These* were the questions Jesus asked when he came in his Advent.

## Repent, the Kingdom of Heaven Is at Hand

*In those days John the Baptist appeared, preaching in the
desert of Judea, [and] saying, "Repent, for the kingdom of
heaven is at hand!" It was of him that the prophet Isaiah had
spoken when he said:*

> *"A voice of one crying out in the desert,
> 'Prepare the way of the Lord,
>    make straight his paths.' "*

*[John said,] "Even now the ax lies at the root of the trees.
Therefore every tree that does not bear good fruit will be cut
down and thrown into the fire" (Mt 3:1-3, 10).*

If we were forced to take stock of our lives, how would things
look? The course of history has seen few individuals like John
the Baptist. But these few force us to evaluate what is true in
our lives and what must be thrown out.

In the eyes of the Baptist, all of the excuses with which we
usually cover up our failures and all our claims that we really
aren't doing anything different from everybody else are worth-
less. We always use the same arguments when we attempt to
explain and legitimate our compromises, our concessions, and
our equivocations: "I just couldn't make an exception," "I don't
have the energy to change my life," "I only know how to act the
way I was taught," "It's just force of habit." All of these expla-
nations are valid in the logic of common sense. But in the logic
of John the Baptist they are what they are, namely, lazy excuses.
Of course we can be different; we don't really need the comforts
of civilization. If it should turn out that living in the land of milk
and honey makes the heart slothful and that the lowing of the
cattle upon the pastures only blocks the ears, then why not go
back into the desert, to the place where Israel knew what it
meant to see God in the column of smoke by day and in the
shape of fire by night? Do we really need all the junk with which
we fill our hands and empty our souls? It was the great hope of

the old prophets of Israel that one could hear and respond to the cry of the needy and the wretched without hesitation. Was Israel herself not once an outsider and a slave in the land of Egypt? Have the people of God completely forgotten what it means to be trampled down and oppressed?

It wouldn't be too difficult to translate what John the Baptist meant into the language of the twentieth century. In the middle of our world of about five billion people, there are more than eight hundred million—one fifth of the world population—who don't know what it means to live. Why is this so? Shouldn't we be upset? Is it possible not to feel what a challenge and a scandal this is? Do we accept it by force of habit? Do we lack the energy to change it? How do we excuse ourselves?

We show each new generation pictures of Auschwitz and Dachau. We even lead them to the actual places so they can see the stones of the ovens and how men and women in the struggle against death dug their fingernails into the walls. Even the hardest and deadest material becomes pliable. Where were our contemporaries then? This question is gouged into the stone. And what are we going to tell future generations when they ask us why we in the northern hemisphere amassed enormous amounts of raw materials and consumer goods, and at the same time were completely unmoved by the misery of millions?

John the Baptist didn't tolerate empty phrases and excuses. He knew very well that only laziness and fear prevent us, even today, from beginning a new life. Against laziness, John used the barb of accusation and reproach, spoken from the mouth of God. Against fear, however, he used the language of fear itself, just as firefighters set backfires to cut off and control a raging brush fire. Thus John stands on the Jordan preaching catastrophe against the catastrophe of human petrification that had already occurred. He couldn't possibly say it more clearly. If everything continues as it is, we will see that God has already laid the ax to the roots of the tree. John already sees the one who will come after him. In John's vision he already has the winnowing fan in his hand, and he will strike with the thresher upon the threshing floor to separate the wheat from the chaff. John speaks the truth clearly and plainly. He points out what has to be done—repent—strongly and urgently. But only when we understand the truth of John the Baptist can we take another step and understand that even this truth, spoken in the middle of Advent, is merely preliminary.

Jesus came as John had prophesied, but he knew that men and women can't be saved with a winnowing fan, thresher, and fire. Fear can't be used against fear. Rather, he sought to soothe the heart that clings to possessions in which it is suffocating, to relax the cramped grip of hands that clutch all the useless things, the renunciation of which would make us much richer than if we possessed everything. He sought to banish the nightmare of fear from the soul so that it would become possible to open the eyes to the misery of others. And he sought to speak, as quietly and gently as possible, to the heart of Jerusalem, so that it would open its ears and hear the cry of the needy.

The truth of John the Baptist can only be lived by means of the message of love. There was a time when the whole of Judea went out to the Jordan desiring to repent and begin a new life. What prevents us today from doing this?

## Dreams and Visions

*The beginning of the gospel of Jesus Christ [the Son of God].*
*As it is written in Isaiah the prophet:*

*"Behold, I am sending my messenger ahead of you;*
  *he will prepare your way.*
*A voice of one crying out in the desert:*
  *'Prepare the way of the Lord,*
  *make straight his paths.'"*

*John [the] Baptist appeared in the desert proclaiming a*
*baptism of repentance for the forgiveness of sins. People of the*
*whole Judean countryside and all the inhabitants of Jerusalem*
*were going out to him and were being baptized by him in the*
*Jordan River as they acknowledged their sins. John was*
*clothed in camel's hair, with a leather belt around his waist.*
*He fed on locusts and wild honey. And this is what he pro-*
*claimed: "One mightier than I is coming after me. I am not*
*worthy to stoop and loosen the thongs of his sandals. I have*
*baptized you with water; he will baptize you with the holy*
*Spirit" (Mk 1:1-8).*

"The beginning of the gospel of Jesus Christ." These words
are emblazoned at the beginning of the gospel of Mark. This is
actually what we *have* to know; namely, how salvation comes to
us.

Whenever we wish to calm ourselves by contemplating the
great figures of history, we tend to focus on the way their lives
ended. When we know how a story ends, we can lean back and
relax. Tension subsides when we know the ending. In real life,
however, we have to pay attention to the beginning, where nothing is yet decided, where every risk is still open, where every
existential possibility is undefined. We remain expectant, hoping, yearning, doubting; we stretch with the entire tension of our
life into the future.

During Advent we are expectant and searching. In a certain

sense this is our whole life—to hope and to believe that what is
essential is coming—for the event that decides everything can
only happen to those who seek it. Thus John's greatest concern
is to make us ready, shake us to attention, and awaken a new
yearning within us.

What are we waiting for? Since the days of John the Baptist
that question is addressed to every person at every time. Old
prophecies about our life on earth are pressing toward fulfillment. But how can we perceive the faded script of God in our
hearts? How do we get in touch with the great and essential in
us?

The message of John the Baptist connects to the longing of
the old prophets of his people after centuries of disregard. The
great figures of Israel, Amos, Hosea, and Jeremiah were convinced that it was necessary to teach the people a new thirst and
a new hunger. Today this theme is perhaps more pressing than
all others. How can men and women be led back to the need
for an almost unknown yearning? The prophets of ancient Israel,
themselves on the brink of despair, believed that if it again
became possible for the people to hear God, then God would
expect them to acknowledge that their way of life was as barren
and desolate as a wasteland. There is perhaps no greater danger
for humanity than to live as we think it our duty to live, externally calm in the satisfaction of every kind of superficial need,
well-supplied, content, well-fed, stuffed to bursting with material
paraphernalia. Beneath, a constantly thickening layer of lead
settles over our souls. We are in danger of forgetting what could
live within us, because we are distracted by the sheer worries
and cares of everyday life.

All of you over fifty at least vaguely remember how things
looked in many parts of Europe after 1945. Entire blocks of
houses were lying in rubble and ashes, people had no money in
their pockets and lived from hand to mouth, but strangely, there
were virtues then that have been lost in the past thirty years,
namely, a feeling of community, of understanding, of readiness
to help each other, to pull together for the same purpose. These
virtues existed before the desert of overabundance that has since
come upon us. We had not yet become bourgeois, we had not
yet become bored, not yet settled down in the land of milk and

honey. As the old prophets would have said, we had not yet given ourselves over to idol worship, fertility cult, and the dance around the golden calf. Or, as we would say today, we had not yet dedicated our lives to empty materialism. At that earlier time, people were able to discern which things were important and which were not. They had a clear and instinctive awareness of what furthers life and what kills. That's why the prophets raved on and on about returning to the desert and living as Israel had once lived. The people didn't know what they would live on the next day, but when they awoke they collected strange food from heaven, piece by piece. They didn't know what it was, and so it was named *manhu*, or, "what is this," that is, the food which comes from God. But in this time of insecure provisions, lack of protection, and constant journeying, the Israelites were generous and near to God. They dared not take a single step without seeing God before them in the column of smoke by day and in the column of fire by night. And it was sufficient to know that God's wings were spread over them and that God travelled side by side with them. What does a man or woman need other than this in order to live?

John the Baptist takes this very seriously when he renews the ritual of baptism—which we tend to misunderstand moralistically. Come and be baptized, he says. A wonderful symbol. Today when a child is born to Christian parents, they bring it to the church to be baptized. They mean to say thereby that a human being, who comes into this world, need never feel that he or she is merely a product of the parents, of the environment, and of extrinsic expectations. The child should be an individual; it has its own identity, which has come forth from the invisible hand of the creator. He or she should be a being whose forehead touches heaven and whose heart is free for God. This is how the child should be able to live. And the child should receive its name in a holy place. For all the prophecies, all the promises, and all salvation of the earth are for him or for her. No one should ever be allowed to dull the pure light of God in the child's heart. No one should ever have the power to block or mislead this child on its way back to the stars. This is what it means to baptize a child.

But what does baptism mean when it is received by an adult,

a person already thirty, forty, or sixty years old? What if it means
a person could recover those forgotten paths, the ones he or she
never travelled? Do you have the courage to imagine how your
life would look if you could begin once again from the beginning? Looking back, with the knowledge you have today, how
would you live, if you could start anew? Most of you are saying:
"Nonsense! To think about such things is troublesome, bewil-
dering, and confusing. We live as we live. The train has left, we
are sitting in it, and we already have twenty or more stations
behind us. We don't even know what line we're on, whether
we're going to Hamburg, London, or Washington. The important thing is that we go on." If this is indeed the way things are,
then John the Baptist doesn't have anything to say. Turning
around is an illusion. Circumstances will drive us on and we
won't be able to hear anything more about God's salvation in
our lives.

But there are many things that we never dared to dream.
There are many hopes that we hardly dare to imagine. In their
place stands the power of resignation, the power of established,
mechanical fear, and the training into which we have been
pushed and which forces us farther and farther away from ourselves. What if we could recover our original form? What if we
could literally turn everything around and begin again at that
point where a genuine experience of life was broken off? What
if that which was lost could sprout up, where it was sown in our
hearts but never flowered? What if it could come forth into light
and beauty? We are much richer then we believe. Our souls are
much more beautiful than we think. We are full of possibilities.
Who or what is it that forces us to renounce them? Only fear,
the lack of confidence, the phrases we have been taught, repeating what the others say and do.

Miraculously, John the Baptist so fascinated all of Judea and
Jerusalem that the people came out of their apartments, their
holes, their caves in the desert to the Jordan. They saw a
vision—that life can begin again, flawless and pure. They didn't
see moral violations or sins in the sense of transgressions of
precepts; rather, they saw that they were being untrue to their
own being, unfaithful to the wholeness of life to which all people
have been called. To confess this and, wherever possible, to

remedy it—this is a great task. But in this way our humanity matures, our happiness grows, and the undistorted form of that which we really are begins to live.

Certainly we can say that this man on the Jordan makes us afraid. He looks too ascetic. We don't want to have anything to do with garments made of camel's hair or food consisting of grasshoppers and wild honey. This is too hard, too absolute; it cuts into our comfort, contradicts our habits, and repels us. Nevertheless, it is necessary in order to discover, beneath all our bourgeois covering, the deeper hope that rests in us all. When we don't lie to ourselves we find a greater happiness than that which we try day and night to talk ourselves into. Perhaps the only question of Advent is how we can teach and communicate to a whole generation, and to ourselves—people in the middle of this human emaciation, withering, and desolation—the courage to set higher goals, to believe in the stars, and to yearn for the heavens. The first stirrings of a feeling for God in our hearts give rise to a thirst and hunger in the middle of a world that does not satisfy us.

No one knew this better than John the Baptist. After him there will come one who does not need to be proclaimed with warnings, cries in the desert, with threats and demands. A longing will arise in our hearts all by itself. For the real miracle of our humanity is that we are baptized with a spirit who lives in our hearts; a holy spirit who grows in our dreams, in our feelings, and in our thoughts; a spirit living in us, not an alien spirit, but the fulfillment of the prophecies of the Hebrew Scriptures. *At the end of time it will be that I will give dreams to the sons and visions to the old men.* Can we believe that this is true? Can we believe there is a new generation inspired by dreams, fantasy, poetry, creativity, and the courage to transform the world according to new standards, new visions? Can we believe there are old people looking back upon their lives as upon a book written by God, beginning to discern the hidden shape that has grown in the few decades of their lives, and seeing before them the promise of eternity beyond death and the grave? The young have their dreams and the old have their visions, and every one of them is baptized in the spirit. What a promise!

## Make Straight His Paths

*In the fifteenth year of the reign of Tiberius Caesar, when
Pontius Pilate was governor of Judea, and Herod was tetrarch
of Galilee, his brother Philip tetrarch of the region of Ituraea
and Trachonitis, and Lysanias tetrarch of Abilene, during the
high priesthood of Annas and Caiaphas, the word of God
came to John the son of Zechariah in the desert. He went
throughout [the] whole region of the Jordan, proclaiming a
baptism of repentance for the forgiveness of sins, as it is written
in the book of the words of the prophet Isaiah:*

> *"A voice of one crying out in the desert:*
> *'Prepare the way of the Lord,*
>    *make straight his paths.*
> *Every valley shall be filled*
>    *and every mountain and hill shall be made low.*
> *The winding roads shall be made straight,*
>    *and the rough ways made smooth,*
>    *and all flesh shall see the salvation of God' "* *(Lk 3:1-6).*

Luke introduces the story of the public workings of Jesus with
extraordinary detail. He prefaces the activity of John the Baptist,
the forerunner of Jesus, with exact details about the various
rulers and their territories. This literary style was usual in
ancient times—it is certainly a technique that follows the style
of the chronicles of the time—yet we probably recount the
essential events in our own lives in much the same way. When
we look back upon a decisive event in our lives, we also tend to
describe it in the greatest detail. We know the hour and the
place, we see the waiting room, the conference hall, the street
almost exactly as it was. We can describe the decor; we know if
the sun was shining on that day or if there was a cold wind
blowing. Every detail is present to us, and yet the decisive
moments in our lives occurred completely independent of all
these things.

We can assume that at the time of John the Baptist the names of all these men were on everybody's lips. From the historical point of view they appeared to be important; they had power; they had control. But still, the decisive event occurred completely apart from them, in a forgotten corner of their realm and in a zone they didn't even consider worthy of patrolling. They, the powerful, suddenly appear upon the stage of history as mere bystanders. They planned and directed the course of world events, but the essential event passed right by them, occurring beneath the level of their vision. It is always so when we are possessed by the conviction that everything depends on us, that *we* are the ones, that *we* must provide a plan. Then the essential event will appear quietly and unobtrusively, a sudden and complete surprise, and all of our intentions will be nothing but stage props, never the driving force that brings it forth.

Does this mean we need not prepare for the decisive event, that it doesn't depend upon us at all? No, indeed! John was called into the desert to prepare. The prophets of the Hebrew Scriptures associate a peculiar vision with this zone of silence. It is remarkable that in the history of religions all the founders of great religions, as if intentionally, sought out places in the desert. In fact, it is the region of truth. The desert is relentless; it is a place almost inimical to life. In the desert only those who are spiritually strong survive. It is a place of endless loneliness, crass interplay of opposites, nights of trembling cold and days of shimmering heat; it is a study in extreme contrasts, the motionless zone of death, the zone of shifting sands, the transitory, with a few oases of exploding life. At every turn the desert forces a decision. It tolerates nothing superfluous; it allows no luxury. It cuts out the unnecessary under the constant coercion of the grating wind. Plants that live there have to adapt by shrivelling their leaves until they become prickly thorns. And the thoughts of men and women form themselves and finally become clear by dropping away all that is useless. Only essential questions are allowed in this zone of silence, and only one single experience accompanies the men and women of the desert day and night; namely, that human beings are small and transient, that the world is endless and great, but that above it there spreads the eternal dome of God's majesty. To look up to God, to live under God's splendor, to seek the paths of the stars, to find ways through the unimaginable, and, above all, to be thankful to stand in God's service and under God's guidance—this is what all the religions of the desert have taught. The lonely men and women of the desert serve ultimately as road signs for humanity.

Thus John the Baptist. That's how the prophets want it. They tell the people of Israel in the middle of the land flowing with milk and honey that they are not merely in danger, but that they must already hear the indictment for having stopped their ears and having allowed their hearts to become lazy. The prophets hoped that God would lead the people back into the desert, to the time when they awoke every morning hardly knowing how they would survive the day. But they *did* survive, by the hand of God, who every morning sent manna upon the earth for the people to gather. Each day came forth from the grace of God. The prophets yearned that men and women would again feel thankfulness and trust; they thought the people would be happier if they lived simply and didn't warp their being with all kinds of ornaments and accoutrements that only seduce the heart and distort the truth. That's why John goes back to the place of prophecy, to the place where Israel received its first lessons and guidance. For only in a simple and undistorted life will we learn to find our way back to the divine origins. There, John used the important word and symbol of baptism and conversion, the image of a new beginning in a guiltless life, so purified, so unblemished as only the desert can teach us to be.

If we now ask what we should do to renounce sin, then this old picture of fulfilled prophetic speech shows us the answer. We must prepare a way for the Lord. Who would not want to do this? Who does not want God to find a path into his or her life? But how? These metaphors come from a time when the remnant of the people of Israel returned from exile and saw that a straight and royal path through the desert had been prepared for them. But how does this picture apply to our lives? It tells us that what is bent should be made straight. It is a brilliant formula for simplicity—not, however, for simplification. In real life things are not as they are in a geometry book, where the shortest distance between two points is always a straight line. In real life we cannot go straight to the goal. We are surrounded by obstacles. We cannot tunnel through or level every mountain. We have to wind around the slope like a snake and make a thousand detours. But our fellow human beings should not be like the mountains which block our passage. Nor should we deal with other people by pushing them aside or trying to wind around them. Those who always go around and bend to the wind will end by themselves becoming serpentine — false, warped, avoiding everyone, and without character.

What is bent should be made straight. This means to dare to speak the truth, to stand up for what we think, not to bend that truth out of fear. On this path others are our partners, not obstacles. Others do not stand in our way like mountains, to be avoided or overcome; they are companions along the way. It doesn't pay to avoid them. What pays is clarity and honesty. And at every point where we avoid the lie and are straight, we prepare a way for God to enter our life. The psalms never tire of praising those men and women whose hearts are straight. The straight thinkers, the clear-headed, prepare a way for God in this world. And the same is so when transposed and applied to the deformations on the vertical plane between peak and canyon, between heights and depths. Our moods and feelings will always run quickly up and down. There will be moments of triumph and times of humiliation. We can't avoid this, even if we try. But we don't have to accept a philosophy that divides life into moments of exhilaration and depression, into highs and lows. For if we do this, we banish ourselves into the hard labor of thinking we have to do it all ourselves.

It is better to take life with equanimity, in a balanced way, more smoothly. When we take problems less seriously, the high mountains don't seem quite so high, the mass of obstacles confronting us doesn't appear so momentous. We know that our lives are not limited to this earthly terrain. The heavens are more important, for against the background of the heavens, the canyons, mountains, and hills of the world are relatively insignificant. And if we force ourselves to divide everything into higher and lower, then many people will appear too large for us and we will be compelled to fight them, and others will appear small and we will disdain them. When we do this often enough, we discover in our hearts much that is small and contemptible, and we try to deny it. Of course, we also find other things that we want to raise up higher, but we won't succeed. We should be even-tempered; the psalms often express this by speaking of the heart which has become small and which no longer looks to the heights. This is the best way to avoid a fall. To level mountains and fill up canyons does not mean making life boring. It means to draw ourselves into a center where life becomes calmer, where life no longer, like the curve of a fever, dances up and down, constantly vibrating and exhausting itself in continual crises, where we are not shaken by euphoria and depression, but come to ourselves in peace.

It is in this desert attitude of simplicity and thankfulness, in the readiness of the heart that is straight, and in the uprightness and directness of the heart that is even-tempered, settled upon the earth, humble and modest, that God finds a path into this world. And wherever this happens, we can see salvation. Where men and women are true, God is present.

## Open Your Eyes and Ears

*"A voice of one crying out in the desert:*
*'Prepare the way of the Lord,*
  *make straight his paths.*
*Every valley shall be filled*
  *and every mountain and hill shall be made low.*
*The winding roads shall be made straight,*
  *and the rough ways made smooth,*
*and all flesh shall see the salvation of God' "* (Lk 3:4-6).

The figure of John the Baptist stands at the beginning of
Advent. He brings a new form of promise and a new form of
hope. For centuries Israel had to comfort herself with what had
been handed down by the fathers; no fresh word of God was
heard. In fact, the conviction that human beings are capable of
seeing and hearing God with our hearts had perished. Instead,
a learned, interpreted, traditional form of religion had arisen,
in which men and women were told in every detail what they
had to believe and do by the scribes and high priests. A life such
as this may be diligent and conscientious and in a certain sense
righteous and faithful, but it is always dry, stale, and empty, a
wasteland of the heart. For the old prophets, the desert was an
image of salvation. The prophets saw how Israel settled down
in the promised land and gradually lost sight of the origin of its
hopes and a feeling for their nearness. Israel no longer could
see and hear God. One can be poor amid external wealth! The
prophets wanted to change this; they even predicted that, when
the time of disaster came, God would drive the people back into
the desert, as in the days of the fathers.

Isn't it always so? We are able to believe strongly in God and
feel God within us when all the guarantees of life, the bases of
our false security, melt away. Israel had once depended on God
for everything. It had thrown off the yoke of slavery and found
itself again upon the other side of the Red Sea. They got up in
the morning and *didn't know* what the day would bring. How
can human beings live like that? Yet it was the time when Israel

was protected the most by the hand of God, a God who went before them by day in the form of a column of smoke and by night as a column of fire to protect them from the burning heat of the sun and to guide them in the darkness of the night. There was no certainty. People received daily whatever they needed in order to live directly from the hand of God. They gathered manna from among the stones and learned to live from hand to mouth, continually, day to day, year to year. In the eyes of the prophets, this alone is real life; a life in constant hope, always moving on, always restless, always sustained by God.

For John the Baptist the prophetic dreamland of the desert was the only possible place from which to speak to the men and women of his time. An entire people waited hundreds of years to be addressed by God. And then, finally, it happens at a certain time, under the rule of people who don't have anything at all to do with it, who don't understand it and haven't organized it and who simply stand around like spectators, or opponents, upon the stage of history, without even faintly knowing what it's all about. Now, presumably God does not speak only at certain times, now and again, and leave us hanging and wriggling the rest of the time for reasons we don't understand. Presumably God speaks to us always, shines constantly, just as the light of the sun is constantly present. Occasionally, there are men and women who see this. The question is how we too can open our hearts so that the all-encompassing truth reaches us. What the prophets tell us is seldom something other than what we ourselves could clearly enough feel and understand. The great figures of the history of religions are not great discoverers and inventors of unheard-of novelties; they are simple people who hear when God speaks to them. They let God come close, and because they are simple enough, they do exactly what God tells them to do.

From the point of view of the Christian Scriptures, John the Baptist may well be a preliminary figure. He wanted the people to *just once* follow the law in the sense in which the old prophets and the original faith of Israel prescribed. His belief is full of longing, clothed in the images of myth that the world would be in order again, that the messiah, the kingdom of God would come, if only Israel would celebrate the Sabbath without sin one

single time, if only once not a single divine precept would be
neglected, if Israel would change its ways, repudiate sin, and
travel the straight path of holiness. And John does not hesitate
to threaten what will happen if the people do not change. God
is breathing down his neck, making him afraid; for John, God
is promise. The words of the fathers are crowding close around
him; it's now or never. Luke, however, takes up John's words in
such a way that the prophecies of Isaiah come to the fore, and
these are pictures beyond constraint, anxiousness, and fearful
righteousness. These are pictures of how we can turn the desert
of our lives into a place where we can welcome God.

For this, it is necessary to make crooked ways straight again.
And we know a lot about this. We spend our days in endless
maneuvering and detours. When did we last have the courage
to tell someone something plainly and directly? When will we
again have the power to deal with something in an honest way?
We twist and turn and wind our way around the truth. How
much courage it takes to give up all the sidestepping of diplo-
macy, which we think necessary to deal with each other, and to
say what we really think, feel, and want! For Isaiah, straightness
of the heart is God's royal road.

And it's exactly the same with the evasions we make. Here,
we need to fill in the valleys. But how often in life do we feel
ourselves thrown into an abyss, beaten down, pressed to the
ground, held captive in a realm of shadows and sadness? How
can we climb out of this, again see the light and return, so to
speak, to ourselves, to being what we really are, living without
the burden of constant disappointment and despair? It would
be enough simply *to be* and to stand with both feet upon the
ground.

And it is no less true with the mountains. How often do we
climb up to the heights, thinking we can only begin to live when
we behave extravagantly? It can't be high enough, big enough,
or waste enough energy!

It is possible to live simply and straightforwardly upon the
plain earth. This would mean that in the midst of truth, the
desert of life could begin to bloom and become rich and the joy
of waiting for God could flower. For God is near. It is only
necessary to open oneself in order to see and hear.

# Third Week
# of Advent

## God's Promises

*When John heard in prison of the works of the Messiah, he sent his disciples to him with this question, "Are you the one who is to come, or should we look for another?" Jesus said to them in reply, "Go and tell John what you hear and see: the blind regain their sight, the lame walk, lepers are cleansed, the deaf hear, the dead are raised, and the poor have the good news proclaimed to them. And blessed is the one who takes no offense at me."*

*As they were going off, Jesus began to speak to the crowds about John, "What did you go out to the desert to see? A reed swayed by the wind? Then what did you go out to see? Someone dressed in fine clothing? Those who wear fine clothing are in royal palaces. Then why did you go out? To see a prophet? Yes, I tell you, and more than a prophet. This is the one about whom it is written:*

*'Behold, I am sending my messenger ahead of you; he will prepare your way before you.'*

*Amen, I say to you, among those born of women there has been none greater than John the Baptist; yet the least in the kingdom of heaven is greater than he"* (Mt 11:2-11).

The question John addresses to Jesus from his prison cell is deeply disquieting: "Are you the one who is to come?"
John had committed his entire life to proclaiming that cer-

tain hopes were about to be fulfilled. He was so convincing and persuasive, so uncompromising, that people from all over Judea streamed to the Jordan. He had the courage to witness to God before the mighty, and now he sits in prison facing certain death. This must have been a hard time for John. Not that he doubted what he had proclaimed. But he must have asked himself if someone had already come, now, in his lifetime, who would fulfill what he had promised, or how long it would still be. He was certain that he hadn't been mistaken about the essence of his promise, but perhaps God would make the people wait and wait, the fate of other prophets throughout the centuries.

The word about Jesus reaches John in prison. And one last time he asks what his prophecy is worth and, in a certain sense, what he should think about himself and his vocation. It is strange that in our lives we do all we can and all we should to fulfill our destinies and, nonetheless, the final judgment of the value and significance of what we did and accomplished comes from outside, from the further course of history, from the hand of God.

What had John been waiting for? For the coming of the kingdom of God, now, in his lifetime, soon. He had told the people how it would be. After him, there would come someone greater then he, someone far more terrible and frightening. The one sent by God would be like an ax laid to the roots of a tree, like fire in straw, like the winnowing fan upon the grain.

Is Jesus the one who fulfills such prophecies? We see and hear nothing of axes, fires, and winnowing fans in the mouth of Jesus. And still he gives the messengers John sent to him an answer, although not a simple yes or no. A *yes* would mean John was right in all the details of his prophecy, and this was not so. A *no* would mean that his prophecy was entirely wrong, and this wasn't the case either. So Jesus tells John's messengers to report what they themselves see and hear. What you see yourself, what you hear yourself—ponder this and ask yourself if it comes from God or not. Is this the salvation that you have been waiting for? Jesus speaks a very quiet language here. These are like words spoken through the bars of the prison. But the list he gives—the blind see, the lame walk, and so on—would have reminded everyone of the words of Isaiah, chapter 35, that when salvation comes, God will heal every misery of the people.

The blind see. How many people are there who, out of misery and despair, see the world in broad daylight as if shrouded in darkness and night, who are blind to the next step they should take? How can such people be given courage, confidence, and a perspective for the future in this life? What Jesus preaches gives men and women the faith to raise their eyes and look ahead.

The lame walk. This we also know. We know how heavy the feeling of hopelessness makes our limbs, as if our entire body were nothing but resignation and sluggishness, as dense as lead. We don't even dare to raise a hand. It is as though we never had the chance to do something meaningful, as though we were never capable of making ourselves happy. But this power must have been present in the preaching of Jesus, because he awakened in men and women the excitement of life and gave them the conviction that it was worthwhile to take their lives into their own hands again.

The sick are healed. There is a very widespread disease that brings people to the point where they think of themselves as contaminated and ill, as something about which others must be warned, as something to be pointed at from afar and branded filth, scum, and trash. Every feeling of guilt has this power to transform men and women into outcasts. But the message of Jesus must have had the power to fill people with the conviction that they were pure and good, acceptable to others, and that they had a right to show themselves again in public and not to fear nearness and companionship.

The deaf hear. How often do we prefer simply to close our ears to the noise of the world? How often do we feel that every meaningful word is buried under a barrage of phrases and that we can see neither meaning, nor understanding, nor purpose in what is said? It's not that we are physically incapable of hearing and registering the sounds being made; it is rather that our ears are plugged with screeching, shrieking, and uproar. There must have been something in Jesus' preaching that made people attentive to others, that made men and women receptive and capable, even amid the din, of hearing delicate words, and that gave them the ability to learn again the joy of melody, of being able to speak, of the community of speech.

Almost like a summary of every need, Jesus adds that the dead are raised to life. There are people who expect from the time they come into the world to see the angel of night rather than the light of day. For them, death always seems nearer than life, as though they were destined never to come forth from the dark caverns of decay and the graves of the earth into the sunlight. The message of Jesus must have made life so attractive that people had the courage thankfully to praise God as the source and origin of life. Jesus preached this message to the poor, for it is precisely they who understand it in the middle of their misery.

But it is questionable whether this gentle and mild message will disappoint John, or whether he will understand it as a new promise, a new calling. So Jesus adds, Blessed is he who takes no offense. It is possible that John is embittered, for everything he prophesied was extremely demanding, terrifying, ascetic, and trying. If now salvation should so softly come into the world, would this not be reason enough to protest that this *cannot* be salvation? John also has to decide for himself what he accepts as truly human and divine in his own life and in his own message.

Then Jesus turns to the people. They also must know who they sought out upon the banks of the Jordan and who now stands before them. Jesus reminds them of their real motivation. They were not baptized by John in order to follow a special attraction or fashion of the moment. It was not a matter of coming to see a weather vane or a reed swaying in the wind. John was not one to vacillate — and everybody knew it. It was also not a matter of participating in some trendy happening so that at the next get-together they could tell everyone all about how they were *also* at the Jordan, the way we tell others at a party that we *also* vacationed in the south. If this were what it was all about, then they wouldn't have had to go to the Jordan. People interested in these kinds of things stay where the money and the power is. This was not John. But when we understand his greatness, we also see his limits. And the most wonderful thing about the way God deals with us is that when God fulfills promises, the result is endlessly greater than we dared to hope, and even that which seemed most true to us appears like an error. The kingdom of God is here and it lives, for the dead are raised to life.

## Speaking with Trust in God

*When John heard in prison of the works of the Messiah, he sent his disciples to him with this question, "Are you the one who is to come, or should we look for another?" Jesus said to them in reply, "Go and tell John what you hear and see: the blind regain their sight, the lame walk, lepers are cleansed, the deaf hear, the dead are raised, and the poor have the good news proclaimed to them. And blessed is the one who takes no offense at me."*

*As they were going off, Jesus began to speak to the crowds about John, "What did you go out to the desert to see? A reed swayed by the wind? Then what did you go out to see? Someone dressed in fine clothing? Those who wear fine clothing are in royal palaces. Then why did you go out? To see a prophet? Yes, I tell you, and more than a prophet. This is the one about whom it is written:*

*'Behold, I am sending my messenger ahead of you; he will prepare your way before you.'*

*Amen, I say to you, among those born of women there has been none greater than John the Baptist; yet the least in the kingdom of heaven is greater than he" (Mt 11:2-11).*

With the words of this gospel passage, it appears that we are standing at a turning point in the history of religions, and also at a turning point in our own view of life. It's as though two principles confront each other in the person of John the Baptist and in the person of Jesus. Each embodies a different point of view. John stands for the peak of what men and women are able to do for themselves when they take life seriously and are responsible to God. After centuries of learned talk about God, an inner vision and intuition begins again to become effective with John the Baptist. God is so immediately present and so penetratingly near for the man on the banks of the Jordan that the people of his time are fascinated by him. When John speaks of God, he feels God's compelling presence. It's now or never. The will must exert all its effort to doing the truth. His preaching consists of simple instructions. He who has two cloaks should give one to someone who has none. If people hesitate to do what he demands, he goads them with the whip of fear by painting terrifying pictures of the one who will follow him, the promised messiah. The Promised One is ready, John proclaims, to lay the ax to the roots of the tree, mercilessly to separate the good from the bad, like wheat from chaff; he will thresh upon the threshing floor and burn what is useless in eternal fire.

Legend tells us that John was brave enough to defend justice and truth at the court of the king by openly accusing him of adultery and corruption. He risked his life for this. From his prison cell he now asks how much his hope, the hope he had held for certain, is being fulfilled and who it is who is carrying this out. Is Jesus the one to whom John had wanted to point?

It is an odd answer Jesus gives. Nothing remains in the message of Jesus of Nazareth of all that was threatening, frightening, and judgmental in the preaching of John the Baptist. The Christian Scriptures hide as well as they can the sensitive break between these two great figures of the Bible, the Baptist and the man from Nazareth.

In reality, the preaching and the person of Jesus are very different from John. Jesus knew that it doesn't help people ' 'hen they are reproached in the name of morality or of the law  The problem is not that they don't have enough good will. Nor oes it help simply to cajole them with pressure and precept, tu tell them they must immediately make an effort to get control over themselves and set themselves upon the right course. Human beings are too helpless, vulnerable, and weak for this. This is what Jesus must have seen, when he again and again felt himself strongly attracted by those who suffered greatly and when he attended to them; in this way he came to see the world with the eyes of those who wept the most. The whole world becomes different for a person who takes this point of view. Nothing looks the same as before. The normal order of things is turned upside down, and the only question that remains is how to help people. It's so simple to talk about clear principles, to say this is good and that is bad. This is correct and that is incorrect. Everything is clear, reliable, certain—but human life is *not* clear, reliable, and certain; it is full of unanswered questions. No real problem of human existence can be answered with such superficiality. And this is the task that Jesus sets himself—to enable men and women to become whole and capable of doing the good that lies dormant within them and that they want to realize. It is an amazing list of events that Jesus invites the disciples of John the Baptist to report out of their own experience—the blind see, the lame walk, and so on. It is like the fulfillment of a prophecy when he bids them to report his healing acts to John the Baptist.

The blind see. How much since our childhood have we not been allowed to see? As soon as a child sees something considered inappropriate, he or she is ordered to see the world differently and not in the way it truly appeared. We aren't allowed to trust our own eyes when this would disturb things or bring them into question. We are required to take the point of view that is proper and prescribed. By the age of ten these blinders, blinkers, constrictions, and forced falsifications of perception distort our vision to the point of blindness. There is much that could shine in our eyes—inner joy, the radiant depths of the soul, a wealth of discovery and curiosity, enterprise, and openness. But where do we see eyes like this, eyes with the enchanting gleam of the heart, open and receptive to all that makes men and women suffer? People who are happy have no reason to flee pain. They can accept it without feeling threatened by it. For them the world does not become a world of interminable duties, of merely looking on or looking away. They are, if you will, the realists, or better, the surrealists of perception, for they see what stands behind things, the motives and the feelings out of which things happen. We human beings have the gift to see with the eyes of poets. But who will unbind our eyes and heal our blindness? And how much encouragement do men and women need before they can begin again to trust their own ability to perceive reality and truth? How can they learn to open their eyes to all things? How can they find the power once again to let *everything* come near and enter into their view, to remain open to the limit of the horizon? This is what the deeds of Jesus of Nazareth must have been like. When he touched the eyes of a blind man, the ability to see truly was given back to him.

Jesus could make the lame walk again. Paralysis, internal if not external, is an experience we know well. We often feel as though we are unable to control our own bodies, that we are like robots under remote control. Everything we do seems controlled by an external command and an alien impulse. It's as though we have slipped away from ourselves and are being pulled this way and that. Influences and impulses appear then as the field of our activities. We do not live from out of our own being, but like a puppet on strings, exhausted within, enslaved without, literally lame, hobbled by every impulse or by our own will and emotion. And when we are asked how it could come to this, we almost always answer that quite early the right to self-determination was taken from us by means of an external moral law. When are we going to begin to really live? How much confidence is needed before men and women dare again to take their own lives into their hands, before they dare to reclaim their own responsibility and power to act, before they risk going after and making something out of that which they see and want for their own lives? Jesus of Nazareth taught men and women who had lived their lives bowed and bent beneath the burden of foreign authority to stand upright; he taught them to take their own position and walk straight. This is what the miracles of Jesus of Nazareth were like.

Jesus tells us that outcasts were made clean. Almost every culture forces men and women in the name of morality to distinguish between what is pure and what is impure and prescribes what is proper and what is improper with regard to their own bodies and to all kinds of things in the surrounding world. There are noble parts of the body and ignoble parts, those judged beautiful and those considered dangerous, those that may be shown and others that must be covered. We are proud of the one and ashamed of the other. Such doctrines leave nothing whole. Everything is segregated, split up to the point that we feel that we are outcasts. We have to warn others not to come too near. We have to cover ourselves, to hide, to run away. And the worst is that we come to fear the very word we name God, the word *love*. No moral law can solve the problem of people who are outcasts like this. Jesus must have believed that there were no outcasts in a world that God had created. There is indeed much in our lives that never should have been, which lies apart and decays, which is moldy from disuse. There may be many such areas and zones in our lives, but when we accept them and bring them back into use, when we let them back into our lives, they take on their original innocence. That would be a religion according to the taste of the man from Nazareth. We take ourselves beyond the confines of tabu, banishment, and impurity. We go back into that sphere of purity in which God created us. Consider how much faith, humanity, and sensitivity this requires!

And the deaf are given back their hearing. We can also say a lot about this from everyday experience. In the din of superfluous talk we fail to hear so much of what is really going on in another person and which, in the clamor, always remains unheard. What if we learned to hear what is only indirectly communicated, if we became sensitive enough to hear the secret, hidden truth in what other people are saying? What if we could hear their concealed and often disguised feelings? Then our ears literally would be opened for the song, the music that could begin in the life of another person and in our own hearts. We could enter into conversations in which the song of the other would blend into our own melody, as in a concert, and we could relate to one another as in a work of art consisting of melody, tone, and harmony.

What if everything in us opened up? The sum of that which our senses, our experience, our own courage to be comprises would be as though the dead were to begin to live again. It would be the reversal of all things, an event that, presumably, only those who suffer would perceive fully.

Christ is convinced that only the poor will understand what he says. All those who are relatively well off won't need this upheaval of everything. But those who know that it can't go on like this also know that it isn't just a matter of making an effort and becoming stronger and more capable. Rather, it means gaining confidence and the courage to be truthful and to trust in God and his grace, and also of being kind to one another as unconditionally as possible. What is greatest according to the human order is nothing compared to this, a negligible quantity in comparison to the kindness God gives and makes possible for us.

So there remained the question of what John the Baptist would be able to hear and to see. Here is a man who tied himself to a way of hoping, of yearning for the future, and of proclaiming this future in the name of God, and then, when this promised future finally came, it looked completely different from what he expected. Indeed, it was hardly recognizable. This happens to us and our expectations too. Do we have the power then to once again change ourselves, from law to grace, from morality to understanding, from human striving to simple being? Everything John did melts down and collapses under the words of Jesus, but it is not lost. What John wanted comes to pass, but entirely from within. It is not whipped into being with the rod of fear; instead, it grows out of the power of a milder climate.

We do not know what answer John the Baptist gave to the message of Jesus. One thing, however, is certain: John lived what he was able to see. This is why Jesus praises him for his greatness. In the end, God will not examine us and judge us for the truths that we were incapable of knowing. He will examine us and judge us according to the truths that we were well able to know, but often denied out of sheer fright. There is one thing to be said about John the Baptist. Anyone who saw in him a reed in the wind, a weather vane, a bag of hot air, or an opportunist was wrong. This man stood fast and straight on the banks of the Jordan, rooted like a tree in the certainty and clarity of his message. He had nothing to offer that looked like external show and pomp and glory. He renounced any claim to power in the external world. The only power he possessed came from the purity of what he said. He spoke sincerely and honestly. That's why he was a prophet, a person so serious about God that he slapped the religion of his time directly in the face, a person who in a certain sense so loved his people that he often couldn't do otherwise than to hurt them. This is the *beginning* of the way in which God speaks, but it is not the end. It is the preparation for learning a kindness that is real. *This* is the greatest thing of all—the end of the external order, the elimination of violence and coercion in the realm of the divine, a blooming in the light, and the warmth of the eternal.

## What Should We Do?

*And the crowds asked him, "What then should we do?" He said to them in reply, "Whoever has two cloaks should share with the person who has none. And whoever has food should do likewise." Even tax collectors came to be baptized and they said to him, "Teacher, what should we do?" He answered them, "Stop collecting more than what is prescribed." Soldiers also asked him, "And what is it that we should do?" He told them, "Do not practice extortion, do not falsely accuse anyone, and be satisfied with your wages" (Lk 3:10-14).*

What should we do?

This is the question that arises whenever we don't know how to go on. At the end of the road we look for a way out, and the more pressing the need, the greater is our desire for good advice and practical solutions. This is what John the Baptist tries to give. He tells us: Care for others and keep for yourselves no more than you need. Let your freedom find its limit in the wants of others. Protect the defenseless rather than exploiting them. He gives rules for every group and kind of people — businessmen, civil servants, soldiers — and for every class according to its specific situation. We would gain much if we would live according to these words from the man on the Jordan.

John illustrated his message with another image, a wonderful symbol — the kingdom of God. When the kingdom of God comes, he said, it will be something more felt than thought, a perfectly new beginning, and this is something we can't do for ourselves. It is like returning to the dawn of creation, like coming home to the origins of our being. This is the image of baptism. What would it be like if we humans, each one of us, got the chance to start life completely new from the very beginning? Then the question, What should we do?, would be entirely wrong. It contains four mistakes in four words. It is never a matter of a "what," of some *thing*; it is a matter of us as a whole, as human beings. It is also not a matter of "should"; if anything at all should be made new, then it is the freedom to be allowed, the freedom to want, to wish, and to be enabled to broaden the heart. It is also not a matter of what "we" must accomplish; it concerns us as individuals, as distinctive and unique beings, each with his or her own horizon within the world in which God wants to become visible. And least of all is it a matter of "do"; it is a matter of living, of being able to exist, of developing and blooming, of maturing into the natural beauty that lies within us. Perhaps life is so difficult because it was made hard for each of us, in one way or another, from our childhood on, to be original, to live a little bit of spontaneity, and to follow the impulses of the heart, which carry within them so much truth, beauty, and greatness.

The coming of the messiah for John is associated with a certain picture of God that we all know in one form or another. It is a God who stands ready to separate the fruitful from those who do not bear fruit, the wheat from the chaff, and to gather what is good into his barn and to burn what is not. He is already standing there with the ax, and he will cut down the useless tree. These images tell us that if we are to have hope at all, then it can only be a hope beyond the day of judgment and beyond the wall of flame. But is this a human hope? Is this a hope we can live by?

When Jesus came, his problem was not the sort of problem that could be solved with ax and with fire. The gospel of John is right; the problem of human existence is darkness and, one must add, coldness. When Jesus came, his task consisted of thawing out the face of humanity, which was frozen like a snowman. We were brought up frozen into the grotesque image of a human being. And when this image is touched by a breath of warmth, when it begins to melt away, we struggle to maintain and preserve our structure, our frozen contours. But real life lies dormant in the earth and waits upon winter's end, hoping for the first ray of warming sunlight. This is the problem of the human heart; namely, how we can learn again to make contact with the eternal dreams of our soul. Popular traditions tell again and again of princes who travel to distant lands where they must learn to love before they can find their way home again.

Such visions of freedom, happiness, and love lie dormant in every human heart. Each one of us is bound, more than anything else, to live life as fully, wholly, and intensively as possible. This duty—yes, this right—is not derived from established and prescribed laws and regulations. It is not dependent upon the permission of others or upon the surrounding environment. It requires only the courage to live for ourselves. This is really the question of Advent. Again and again we see how fear seems to be stronger than hope, how the force of gravity overcomes the flight of the heart, how inertia is tougher and more crippling than freedom, and how coldness is often mightier than the warmth of love. But why can it not be possible, in the middle of so many broken dreams, destroyed hopes, and disappointed expectations, to make contact again with the power God gave us when he sent us into this world? What should we believe in, if not in the power of love? Without love this earth would be nothing but darkness, inertia, and coldness. What should we believe in, if not in the power of freedom? Without this faith, the earth would be narrow, oppressive, and constricted in armor. And if not in happiness, then in what should we believe? For otherwise the world would be flooded by a sea of tears. We must dare to be ourselves and find the courage to live our own lives. Stop asking, What should I do? Ask instead: Who can I become? Who am I? What is lying dormant in me, waiting for life? We shouldn't be ashamed when that which stirs in us appears unfinished, imperfect, awkward, like a beginner. This is Christmas— the birth of a hope, something very small, a God in becoming, a human being who wants to grow. Those who find this too insignificant will not come to Bethlehem; they will not come out of Jerusalem where the ones who have "made it" live, those who have reached the top and accomplished something, the kings, the leaders, the people with gold and silver jewelry. But humanity begins only where the stars shine in the night, where the wandering star stops and rests, and where, in the middle of poverty, in the middle of the cold, the risk of human existence is hazarded and angels begin to speak.

Occasionally human history creates wonderful symbols and images. Near the coast of southern India there is a small group of islands, the Maldives. Archeological excavations on these islands uncovered temples of the sun left behind several thousand years ago by a people who dared to cross the Persian Gulf with simple reed boats. These seafarers braved the extremes with only one goal before them, to follow the path of the sun. They didn't know that hundreds of miles to the south new islands awaited them, but no sooner had they set foot upon land than they began to build steps, terraces, temples, and galleries that rose upward toward the sky, to the light, to the sun. This is not something others can do for us, but only each one for himself or herself. We should follow our yearning and sail after the light, following the impulse of our need for love no matter how uncertain the horizon may appear. Wherever we land, it will be possible to raise the soul to the heavens and form our lives into prayers that, step by step, climb to eternity.

## Moving Closer to the Kingdom

*And the crowds asked him, "What then should we do?" He
said to them in reply, "Whoever has two cloaks should share
with the person who has none. And whoever has food should
do likewise." Even tax collectors came to be baptized and they
said to him, "Teacher, what should we do?" He answered
them, "Stop collecting more than what is prescribed." Soldiers
also asked him, "And what is it that we should do?" He told
them, "Do not practice extortion, do not falsely accuse anyone, and be satisfied with your wages."...
"[The Messiah] will baptize you with the holy Spirit and
fire. His winnowing fan is in his hand to clear his threshing
floor and to gather the wheat into his barn, but the chaff he
will burn with unquenchable fire." Exhorting them in many
other ways, he preached good news to the people (Lk 3:10-
14, 16-18).*

If we follow the Christian Scriptures, John the Baptist was
the precursor and herald of Jesus of Nazareth. He himself, however, would hardly have seen anything preliminary in the job he
had to do; rather, he would have seen it as something final and
definitive. As he saw it, the time had come for an irrevocable
decision; God stood prepared to have done with the world and
with human history if people did not do what they clearly knew
to be right.

As many others before him in the course of human history,
John also attempted to bring order into human life by appealing
to the good will and the moral sense of the people. From his
point of view, things are quite simple. And as strange as he might
seem to us, eating locusts, calling in the desert for conversion
with thundering words of damnation in his mouth, in one way
he is quite accommodating and familiar to us, namely, he dis-
tinguishes clearly between good and evil, right and wrong, what
is permitted and what is prohibited. When we don't know what
to do, people like John the Baptist are very welcome, for they
show us how to reduce life to simple formulas. So the people

crowd the banks of the Jordan and ask the question that everyone who has ever felt mired down has asked: What shall we do?
John's reply is honest and simple. When Jesus later speaks about
this man, who was actually his teacher, he says that John was
the greatest among all who were ever born of woman. Perhaps
two thousand years later we can better appreciate and understand the concerns and the way of being of this man than his
contemporaries could.

So the people come out to John from the region of Judea and
from Jerusalem, and they ask how they can escape the approaching day of God's judgment. And John answers that if we have
two cloaks, we should give one to someone who has none. And
the same for food. If we today would take John's advice seriously, then we could be certain that much injustice, violence,
and destruction would cease to exist in this world. In a world in
which more than a third of humanity lives in misery, on the edge
of the minimum needed to exist or even below it, the way in
which we have entrenched ourselves upon an island of afflu-
ence — as though we owned it — is a nightmare and a catastrophe.
We only need to compare the commotion and bustle of the last
few shopping days before Christmas with the pictures of misery
and violence we see on television in order to see that this system
is wrong and amounts to permanent injustice. If we were to
share one half of our wealth with the needy, everyone would
presumably have enough. This rule is brilliant and extremely
practical. It would be necessary to get rid of what we don't need
and in times of need, to ask ourselves what really is important
and essential.

Tax collectors also came to the Baptist. These were men who
were considered enemies of the people, traitors, helpers of the
exploitative Roman occupation. They were despised and socially
scorned. It is these men who made the machinery of domination
possible and practical. Although they were Jews, they worked
against the Jewish people, carrying out the work of the enemies
of Israel and blurring the clear front between the two peoples
by their collaboration. They kept the wheels of the system
greased. They were hated by almost everyone. One would think
that a preacher, whose sole concern is God's justice, would con-

demn the tax collectors and declare their entire occupation immoral and unprincipled.

John doesn't do this. He does not force this group of "lost" men to give up their work and face financial or even existential ruin. What he tells them is something quite possible for them to do. They should not add their own private exploitation to that prescribed by the ruling powers. Today, too, it would be an indescribable gain if, in the middle of so-called impasses and dilemmas, we did not become cynical and unscrupulously increase existing injustice on our own initiative. Human history cannot be made right with a snap of the fingers; it may therefore seem suitable to look the other way now and again and not pay too much attention to particulars. A great deal of suffering, injustice, and violence in this world could be avoided by not adding our own injustice to it all.

And it's the same for the soldiers. We would like to hope for a world to come in which our grandchildren will look back upon the twentieth century and wonder uncomprehendingly why it once was necessary for young people to learn to kill for their nation when ordered to do so. We would like to hope that the generation after the next will look back upon us with the same shudder, the same disgust and revulsion we experience when, for example, we see ethnological films on cannibalism and head-hunting in New Guinea, understanding, perhaps, that the system holding sway there represents an archaic culture, with customs no longer acceptable to more highly civilized people. We might expect John the Baptist simply to prohibit military service and certainly the Roman military, for only Roman soldiers could be meant in this context. Power politics, conquest, subjection of entire peoples — all that should belong to the past in a human history that claims to have anything at all to do with God. At least it should be condemned.

But this is not what John said. He simply told the soldiers that they should not raise the premium of their plundering arbitrarily, or torment those who are defenseless, or appropriate possessions that do not belong to them. Our history would certainly look a lot better if greed and rapacity were at least partially held in check. We have to admit that John the Baptist,

with his realistic, sober goals, is indeed the greatest of all who
were born of woman.

Nevertheless, from the point of view of Jesus, the doctrine of
his teacher is not sufficient. When a person with two cloaks gives
one to the person who has none, good will is not created. Rather
the contrary, it creates despondency, sadness, and depression.
It is not possible to change people merely with clear instructions.
Those of us who ask, What should we do?, are likely to be fairly
well off; we are relatively secure in our own abilities and imagine
we are steering the ship of life on a steady course through the
sea. But the truth is that this ship might find itself in the middle
of a storm. Then it isn't so much a matter of holding a steady
course as of simply surviving. Jesus was much more closely
involved with people who felt themselves driven here and there.
The Pharisees were nearer to John the Baptist, for they knew
how things should be and even wanted to tell others what to do.
For Jesus, the issue was not merely how to get people to do
what is right, but how to get them to find themselves so that
they could perceive their own inner truth.

"Let him give one to the person who has none." In the Sermon on the Mount, Jesus says that when you do good your right
hand should not know what the left hand does. He meant we
should do good as though it were something obvious and unworthy of special notice, not think about it, not make a special goal
out of it, but simply act spontaneously on behalf of those in
need. And accordingly, he describes the judgment day of God
differently from John the Baptist, not as if God will beat the
threshing floor, not as a clear separation of good from evil, but
according to the simple standard of the good. We will always
encounter men and women who, either in the literal or meta-
phorical sense, are prisoners, who are naked, who are hungry
and in distress. And we should automatically reach out to them,
take care of them, give them what they need. At such a time we
needn't think about doing something good, about Jesus Christ
or God or the kingdom of love. We do something very simple,
obvious, and straightforward. For Jesus, it is in such almost forgotten moments that the truth of heaven comes to shine here
upon our earth. Jesus does not bring a new moral law but a

chance to grow in trust, a faith that teaches us to realize in our lives what we truly are.

Finally, Jesus' attitude toward tax collectors is not so much that the amount of exploitation be reduced, or that they should give up their profession, but rather that we become free enough to step out of the entire structure of having and not having. And so, in the Sermon on the Mount he points out the lilies of the field and tells us we are infinitely more beautiful than they. Jesus wants to give us the courage to be able to live simply, beyond the system of domination and oppression. Jesus' question is not how to change the political system all at once, but rather, how we can dissolve the fear we have of one another. And he says that when we are slapped upon the one cheek, we should offer the other. He trusts us to perceive how other people suffer when they do us harm, and what they go through when they think they must walk over dead bodies to reach their goal.

It is true that John the Baptist was the greatest man born of woman, but Jesus adds that he was also the smallest. He was standing only at the beginning, when it comes to God. In the historical sense, John the Baptist probably saw himself as preacher of that which is final and irrevocable. In the essential sense, however, he was preliminary in the way that all questions about what we should do finally dissolve into the question of who we really are. Then we will see why it cannot be a matter of separating the wheat from the chaff; we will know how deeply we are bound up with each other, and how good and evil are inseparably present in our hearts. Then we will begin to hope that God will accept us totally, just as we are, and we will begin to hope that we will become capable of accepting each other in understanding and kindness. And, finally, we will be one big step nearer to the kingdom of God.

## To Begin Again

*A man named John was sent from God. He came for testimony, to testify to the light, so that all might believe through him. He was not the light, but came to testify to the light.*

*And this is the testimony of John. When the Jews from Jerusalem sent priests and Levites [to him] to ask him, "Who are you?" he admitted and did not deny it, but admitted "I am not the Messiah." So they asked him, "What are you then? Are you Elijah?" And he said, "I am not." "Are you the Prophet?" He answered, "No." So they said to him, "Who are you, so we can give an answer to those who sent us? What do you have to say for yourself?" He said:*

> *"I am, 'the voice of one crying out in the desert,*
> *"Make straight the way of the Lord,"'*

*as Isaiah the prophet said." Some Pharisees were also sent. They asked him, "Why then do you baptize if you are not the Messiah or Elijah or the Prophet?" John answered them, "I baptize with water; but there is one among you whom you do not recognize, the one who is coming after me, whose sandal strap I am not worthy to untie." This happened in Bethany across the Jordan, where John was baptizing (Jn 1:6-8, 19-28).*

No one before John the evangelist dared to describe the figure of the precursor in such modest terms. Everything he reports about this man shrinks to a voice in the desert beyond the Jordan, in the land of death. Others may want to see John the Baptist as the returning Elijah, or even as the messiah himself, but John the evangelist sees in him nothing further than a sign. But of what sort?

We are used to celebrating Advent in the rhythmical routine of the church calendar. It is clear that on December 25 the Word of God descends into the darkness of this world. It is difficult to imagine not knowing all this and to put ourselves in the posi-

tion of the man on the Jordan, who doesn't have anything concrete to go on, just a certain vision, a vague idea of something
which *must* come to pass if life is to begin anew. But isn't this
just what Advent means—to begin everything anew, when possible, even our relationship to Christ? We have grown up within
Christianity, perhaps too much so, for we have been Christians
ever since kindergarten. But how do we really need to live, and
how do we get ourselves to the point where we can once again
ask all those questions necessary in order to prepare ourselves
for Christ and his coming?

In the days of John the Baptist, people thought it would be
necessary to give up everything; this was very hard. This man
on the Jordan didn't believe it was possible to go to the Temple
Sabbath after Sabbath, to continue reading the holy scriptures,
to continue performing sacrifices according to the law of Moses,
and simply encounter God in the ongoing holy days. He thought
it was necessary to leave the holy city, even to forget for a while
the residence of God in the Temple, in order to plant truth in
the hearts of men and women. But how? Is it possible that the
entire history of salvation and everything that the Jewish people
believed would have to be turned back to the beginning, that a
new exodus into no-man's land, without any preparation, would
have to occur? Why would this be necessary?

John seems to think that in his day everything has been talked
to death and that everything has become literally emptied of the
spirit. We should remember that at the time of John the Baptist
and the man from Nazareth more than three hundred years had
passed without prophecy, without anyone who, empowered by
the spirit, spoke of God. One simply rolled the scrolls in and
out and established one commentary after the other about the
will of God. An entire caste of priests and scribes governed and
regulated that which should be a freely flowing fountain of life.
John the Baptist relied upon nothing other than the feeling of
the desert itself. And in this he appears to us extraordinarily
modern. If we take a look around, how do our lives appear?
Who of us is touched by something of the word of God, such
that it comes to a decision between salvation or damnation? And
when we do have a presentiment of what is to come, for what
does it prepare us? Have no fear, the priests and Levites from

Jerusalem will immediately be sent out, and they will run John the Baptist through the usual question-and-answer game typical of all investigative agencies and bureaucratic institutions. Who are you? We *have* to know. We have categories in which everything and everyone have to appear. Are you the messiah? If this were so, if he could fit that label, then the world would be complete and all hopes fulfilled. We could sit back and relax.

But John the Baptist is in no way the end of all expectations. Quite the contrary. He wants to pull down the curtains and run the bad show offstage. He wants to tell us to get involved in something that is coming soon, something over which we have no control and no say at all. It is not the end of all hopes, but the beginning of all expectations. It is longing, need, craving, seeking, and not knowing. And so the first thing he says is that he is not the messiah.

But then he is asked if he is Elijah. The first three gospels put into the mouth of Jesus words that say John is the returning Elijah. Elijah wanted to free his people from idol worship. He fought against the Moloch of the Canaanites, a sham of a god into whose jaws children were thrown so that he could eat them to sustain himself, a loathsome idol. According to Elijah, God should be seen in the form of a human being, not as a monster who devours children. This is something John the Baptist could stand for, but that would make it too easy for the authorities to tie him to Elijah, turning him into an established figure instead of letting him live like a blazing fire. This is not the man on the Jordan. He is not the eruption of the final event, not merely a new piece of information about God, not someone to categorize and put to rest. He is not even the prophet.

Perhaps preparation for Christ must begin in the following way: We should cancel out everything we thought we knew, leaving us with nothing. We should abolish all the language games by which we classify, order, and categorize everything. Then maybe we could openly accept something that never occurred before, something really new and transformative. Then the man on the Jordan would not be merely a historical figure, but he would stand for something that we ourselves should do, not actually an example for us, but rather a path in the middle of the desert. Let him come and give testimony to the light. If it is not possible to say that the real people of Abraham live in Jerusalem and that the true worship of God resides in Israel, and if it is not possible to adore Christ properly within the hard, thick walls of our churches, and if it is not at all clear where God is to be found, then we must surely feel and see that a paralyzing and dark despair is spreading about us today. There is no longer any clear border between lightness and darkness. In the middle of this darkness we are called to testify to the light. The only real preparation for God is to say continually: "I am not the one. I am not the one you expect or want. Your desire exists not in me but in the heart of each man and woman, something like a spark of light that can be fanned with a quiet, warm breath into a blazing fire that shines brightly."

How many people experience life as one great insanity, one vast night of despair and hopelessness? Externally our lives may look quite proper and chic, but where are we going? To testify to the light means to encourage men and women to believe in warmth amid the cold, to trust against the hardening of the heart, to have faith in feelings of insight and hope, of love and passion. To testify to the light means to encourage men and women to place their trust in what is still invisible, even if the sun should hide itself, and to do all this in the middle of the desert. In our times and in our world to speak of God at all is a difficult and uncertain matter. Those of us who speak of God appear to be describing some sociological entity, something we create for ourselves in order to defend our power or to disguise our weakness with illusions. Maybe our talk signifies remembrance of violence suffered as a child. Perhaps to talk about God refers to certain collective ideals. In short, talk about God is talk about something we classify according to sociological, psychological, or political categories, creating a sort of modern form of Elijah, or of the prophet, or of the messiah. When all the classifications are done, there still remains a great deal of spiritual desert, inhumanity, and bewilderment. This has to be true if the first three gospels say that the people who came out to the Jordan were people who didn't know how to go on. They probably best understood what John wanted. He wanted hope in a God who had never been proclaimed in this way, a God who is like water — flowing, supporting, purifying, life-giving, and good — the element that makes fruitful gardens out of wasteland, the beginning of life in the middle of drought, rigidity, and desiccation. How much energy and vitality has been buried in us and must be set free by a new baptism, by a second birth! John the Baptist can only say: I can't do this. I cannot create new life. But it is already a lot at least to know that a true life is possible. Only when we believe in it can we begin to find it within ourselves. Could it be that two thousand years after Christ has come, we have still to learn everything again from the very beginning? I believe this is exactly what Advent means: to begin again from the start, to be born again, to begin again, to be saved.

# Fourth Week
# of Advent

## Dreams of Love

*Now this is how the birth of Jesus Christ came about. When his mother Mary was betrothed to Joseph, but before they lived together, she was found with child through the holy Spirit. Joseph her husband, since he was a righteous man, yet unwilling to expose her to shame, decided to divorce her quietly. Such was his intention when, behold, the angel of the Lord appeared to him in a dream and said, "Joseph, son of David, do not be afraid to take Mary your wife into your home. For it is through the holy Spirit that this child has been conceived in her. She will bear a son and you are to name him Jesus, because he will save his people from their sins" (Mt 1:18-21).*

If there is any text in the New Testament that can bring into question our entire way of believing, yes, our whole religion, then it is this text from the beginning of the Christmas gospel. It talks about the power of dreams to give meaning to our lives and tells of the appearance of an angel of God in the hours of the night. Such ideas are completely foreign to us today. When we encounter God, it is certainly not in the images that appear in our dreams. We only allow ourselves to relate to God by means of clear thinking and carefully planned actions. The kind of spirituality this gospel portrays is so alien to our culture that we have to put ourselves in the place of people from a simpler time and way of thinking in order to understand what is actually meant here.

The chief of the Duwamish, in the area today called New

York, was once asked to sell the land of his ancestors. On this occasion he gave a speech that has become famous. He compared the way of living of the Indians with that of the white man. For him, the decisive difference lay in the kind of religion that the two peoples professed. Your religion, he said, was written upon stone tablets with the iron finger of an angry God, so that you wouldn't forget it. This religion has always been strange to us Indians. We have never understood it and have never taken it into our hearts. Our religion is based upon the dreams of our forebears and the visions of our chiefs and the ways of our ancestors.

The spirituality of these Indians was not dictated from outside under the threat of command and punishment but was discovered within. Indian children were taught to dream of God. They had to prepare themselves, often for weeks at a time, in prayer and solitude in the mountains in order perhaps to receive a dream from the Great Spirit.

We are so far away from this gospel, which prepares for the celebration of Christmas, that when we first hear the story we must deliberately break off our train of thought to avoid drawing (for us) the obvious conclusion. What Joseph dreams during the night is clearly nothing but wish fulfillment. He loves his wife and wants to marry her, but he thinks he has been betrayed. We can be sorry for him; he is a clear-thinking man, a righteous man, and he has to solve his dilemma. He keeps his anger to himself and avoids a public scandal. Possibly, one should translate the text here more sharply: "Joseph was an upright man, *but still* didn't want to disgrace his wife." For there is a contradiction here. A righteous man, an upright man need not love a wife who even before the marriage becomes pregnant by another man. Such a man has to keep silent deliberately, as Joseph did, if he doesn't want the crime to be made known and his beloved to be stoned as the law decreed. Caught in the dilemma, Joseph chooses silence, but he is not entirely satisfied. His heart contradicts his reason. His feelings don't want to believe of the woman he loves what his senses and his reason tell him must be so. It is a conflict between heart and intellect, between love and justice.

We can look to the German stage of one hundred and fifty

years ago in order to get an idea of this conflict. The struggle of opposites is formulated in the work of Heinrich von Kleist. Men and women are torn asunder when their entire longing, their whole sensibility, and the language of their souls stand in contradiction to what they experience outside in the world and to what the laws of reason dictate. People are driven to madness when they are forced to face a conflict such as this. Is there a solution? The heart has its ways, and reason has its own order. How can people live when they are constantly thrown back and forth between two worlds? How can a man like Joseph still believe in righteousness and loyalty when his reason tells him the woman he loves must be judged unfaithful? How can human relationships still be maintained and relied upon if such things are possible? If the law of gravity were suspended on our planet for a while, so that no stone would remain upon another, it would be a lesser catastrophe than the disruption of integrity and reliability among people portrayed in this story. Nothing would be true and valid, even when the external order was rees-tablished by force of punishment. Uncertainty and doubt would remain, and the heart would never again come to rest. Joseph is troubled and unsettled even in his sleep and tortured in his dreams.

All the more reason, we might think, to believe that in his desperation he would have recourse to fantasies, projections, and wish-fulfilling dreams. An angel of the Lord appears to him in a dream. This is a pious invention that has nothing to do with reality—at least this is what our critical reason tells us.

But the same contradiction Joseph experiences affects all of us.

What would happen if we just once had to admit that the language of longing is more correct than the logic of reason? What if the language of the heart is more reliable than the testimony of the senses? What if faith in love is greater than the certainty of external order? Only then would we be moving toward the kind of spirituality that is expressed in this gospel.

It is indeed possible to learn to trust our own heart. It is possible to listen within ourselves so deeply that the certainty of a pure and unmixed emotion appears to us more convincing than everything which comes to us from without. It is possible to believe that human trust is unshakable, even when everything outside seems to contradict it. Love alone possesses the power to accomplish this. It transfigures our experience of the world into a dream world full of magic and poetry. In love external things — trees, flowers, the stars, and clouds — inspire us to dream of the people who are near to us and who we have taken into our hearts. Love teaches us to see the entire world of external things from within, in symbol and parable. And suddenly these things show themselves to be signs of the promise of nearing love. This power possesses the yearning and the unifying power of the heart that is able to sublimate the external world, a world that separates people from one another, into a symbolic bridge of togetherness. Everything can be transformed into a dream-like experience with feelings of gentleness, sharing, and intense reality. For love, dreams are often more real than the reality of the external senses; for love, the perceptions of the heart are more reliable than the reflections of our sense organs. And it is even possible, when we listen deeply enough within ourselves, to hear the silent voice of God, which speaks truth within our being.

How can God be born into this world unless we plunge back into the true nature of our hearts, into the unmistakable certainty of our love, into the never-ending language of our longing? It is only in our hearts that God can really appear, within you and within me. Only when we trust our own feelings enough will God have a chance to take on the form of a man or woman in this world. Each of us has an angel of God by our side, an angel who lives in our love, who is expected in our longing, who appears in our dreams, and whose language is capable of awakening our inmost being, of freeing us from inner captivity, and of liberating all within us that wants to live. At first, what we perceive is an ancient promise, a traditional vision, a message handed down from the ancestors. But Joseph does what the angel in the dream tells him to do. And thus he teaches us an unusual, much truer, deeper form of faith than any we know. If this gospel is true, then faith must mean to discover again and newly confirm in the dreams of our own hearts and the language of our own love the old, handed-down dreams of the prophets, the seers of our ancestors. Then God will speak to us from within, no longer upon stone tablets written with an iron hand, inspiring fear and awe in us so we don't forget his message. God will then speak kindly within the heart of Jerusalem, in order to comfort us.

## Seeing with the Heart

*When . . . Mary was betrothed to Joseph, but before they lived together, she was found with child through the holy Spirit. Joseph her husband, since he was a righteous man, yet unwilling to expose her to shame, decided to divorce her quietly. Such was his intention when, behold, the angel of the Lord appeared to him in a dream and said, "Joseph, son of David, do not be afraid to take Mary your wife into your home. For it is through the holy Spirit that this child has been conceived in her. She will bear a son and you are to name him Jesus, because he will save his people from their sins" (Mt 1:18-21).*

Guided when in doubt, protected when in need, strengthened in hope. Whenever people don't know how to go on in life, so the holy scriptures tell us, angels appear to them and show them the way. It's different for us today. We are without instructions coming from holy dreams, we know nothing of visions of angels, we are left alone with our questions and doubts. But what if the way in which God communicates with men and women in the Bible is no different from the way we experience him today?

What do we really understand about the person standing next to us? What do we know about ourselves? This story from the first chapter of Matthew's gospel tells us it is possible for us to suspect the person we love most of betrayal, deception, and disloyalty precisely in the moment when she gives life to what is most holy and brings our salvation into the world. Our lives are often so contradictory and confused that we turn toward despair precisely when reason for hope is already on the way. What is the truth of human life? If we follow the logic of our intellect and the way we use our reason and our understanding, then we see a world in which we abuse the law, in which we try to get by with lies and excuses, a world in which truth seems absent from our standards and our language. What can we rely on? Earthquakes, storms, and natural catastrophes can be frightening, but the ground beneath our feet is most uncertain and the atmosphere in which we live most dangerous when we can no longer trust our own words and the words of others.

But what if things really happen as this story in Matthew's gospel says? A woman tells the truth, but the testimony of our senses and the evidence of our understanding speak against her. How can we go on living when our reason and perception destroy rather than further life? How can God speak in our lives when we stand ready to banish and condemn? God never changes, and in the time span that we can survey, human history has hardly changed at all. Therefore, we can suppose that God spoke in the first century as he does today. Yet the circumstances confuse us. Is it true that the woman Joseph loves is capable of doing what reason and common sense tell him she did? Is it possible that the requirements of morality are different from the certainty of the heart?

This story, which describes a truth between men and women beyond what can be proved and, in a certain sense, beyond what is reasonable, is one of the most beautiful in the scriptures. Logic and the senses cannot teach us what we really need to know about one another. Rather, there is an immediate language of the heart, which is infinitely nearer to the truth than all the reasons of our minds and the certainties of our eyes. The inner voice and inner feelings provide light in which we see more clearly than in the light of day. And there are dreams that teach us to see the inner nature of another person clearly.

What happens when an angel appears? It is the figure of a power that cannot be grasped, cannot be contained, but which nevertheless lives in our soul. God has something to tell us from out of our own being, and this is the most important thing of all. It means that when we want to learn the truth about another person, we must inquire into ourselves, into the deepest layers of our heart. We must ask what we believe, what our being tells us and what we can see there, without it being distorted by fear from without and confusion within. The Bible describes this as the vision of an angel. We might say it is seeing one another with the eyes of God.

Israel believed that a messenger of God would appear at the end of the world, when the history of the chosen people was near its end. But we need a messenger in our own lives as well. There are truths that we must and can settle only with God,

when the world offers no way to go on. We sense that the hand
of God guides us more strongly from within, hidden, than by
means of all the impressions and events of the external world.
We need to see that which we can only perceive with the heart.
This is what the purity of emotion, the power of trust, and the
poetry of dreams are able to tell us of another person who is
near to us, and it is infinitely more true than the testimony of
the senses and the logic of the intellect. But it is only when we
purify our heart that it is able to stand up to the doubts, the
objections, the dictates of morality and the requirements of reason that separate us from one another. God's faithfulness to us
is unbreakable, and there are ways of togetherness among men
and women that cannot be destroyed.

When we prepare ourselves during Advent for the coming of
our savior, we need to trust and see with our hearts, as Joseph
did. Salvation will only be able to grow in our lives when we
again learn the language of dreams, when we dare to accept
more courageously, openly, and honestly the secret messages of
our hearts, and when we take the certainty of love more seriously
than the doubts and condemnations of reason. God will come
into the world when we begin to forget everything we *think* we
know about the course of things. Our salvation begins in what
is unseen, in the freedom that lies within us, in letting go of the
false ways we have been taught to live. There is something in
our hearts that we must discover and that we long to behold
with the eyes of the soul from all eternity. This unseen thing is
our entire happiness, and our hope binds us to God, for it speaks
the language of love — and this is indestructible.

## The Instructions of the Angel of God

*In the sixth month, the angel Gabriel was sent from God to a town of Galilee called Nazareth, to a virgin betrothed to a man named Joseph, of the house of David. The virgin's name was Mary (Lk 1:26-27).*

The words of the gospel put to the test the way in which we look at life and understand reality. Decisive religious texts are like a general examination of our religious sensibility; in other words, texts concerning angel messengers and virgin birth are difficult to understand.

We listen to the stories about the birth of Jesus as though they were historical texts. But they are not. We are irritated, perhaps because we don't understand, when Joseph encounters and is guided by an angel. When we hear that Jesus was born out of the mystery of God, a virgin birth, we become confused and perplexed. Are we supposed to understand this literally or symbolically, historically or metaphorically, as a physical miracle or as a transformation of the heart? Religious texts are not supposed to confuse us, but they certainly introduce a peculiar disorder of that which we call normal. And so the question here becomes, What happens when *we* encounter an angel? Or, more exactly, not *an* angel, but *the* angel of God—in singular—for there is only one angel. What God says to us in our lives has only one form. Whether we perceive it or not—whether we can follow its instructions or not—this decides our salvation or damnation.

Everything starts with a person who is very important and near to us. Everything we know of this person is based upon our shared experiences. A walk together, a cup of coffee together, or a book read aloud together tell us *what* happened between us, but not what it *means* that it all happened. In order to say who another person really is, we have to say what he or she means to us; in other words, we have to tell what an encounter with this person did to us, how it changed us. This is especially true in religious questions.

When Jesus' disciples say how the encounter with the man from Nazareth affected them, they can only do so by describing the changes in their own lives. In this way they compose a picture of the person Jesus. Such stories, if they are to be understood at all, must be understood purely from within. They are completely different from historical accounts. We call such stories legends. In this particular case we have the story of a legendary birth.

When we were children, we believed in fairy tales and legends and fables. Now, this is no longer true. We know giants didn't create the mountains; now we explain the gigantic forces of nature in terms of volcanic energies in the crust of the earth. The one has got nothing to do with the other. And this is necessary when we want to understand nature. But if we want to understand another person, or even ourselves, we must again turn to the poetic realm of fairy tales, legends, myths, and fables. What does not become a dream from within is not true. What we offer can only offend another person if it does not reflect our soul. And only that which we can appreciate and understand in pictures or in music or in holy writings gives testimony to God. When the angel of God does not appear to us in the presence of another person, enveloping him or her in light and significance, then we have met someone in the usual manner, but we have not met a person sent from God and thus inescapably confronted the issue of salvation or damnation. And thus we should not expect to find historical information in the text about the birth of Jesus; instead, we read a performative text, a text that changes and forms our very lives today. What the text says is true for us today. It is an impulse, in a certain sense, to close our eyes and see an eternal dream of God in our soul. We are touched and changed by the shining power of Jesus of Nazareth reaching into our time.

How can we say that we have experienced Jesus of Nazareth as the incarnation of God? There are many ways of expressing this in the Christian Scriptures. Some say, he has opened my eyes; others say, he gave me back my innocence; and still others say, he set me free from the prison of oppression. All say that their lives were somehow opened up by the encounter. If we summarize all this, then we have to say that, for me, Jesus *is*,

not that he *was*; we have to say that this *is* true for me or that
it will be so, as if I were to be born again of the spirit and from
God. Of course, we all exist on earth because we have a mother
and a father from whom we received our life. This is an explanation that describes why we exist and that more or less says
why it is so difficult for us to be ourselves. Our parents gave us
everything they could—the biological equipment, care, education, a rootedness in our cultural and social environment—and
all this is like a net that encompasses and supports us.

But the question remains, Who are we? What is living when
we are wrapped up in this cocoon spun from the makings and
doings of other people? Biology, psychology, and sociology
explain a great deal, but never what is most important—who we
ourselves really are. They explain the meaning of our names,
but not our individuality. To discover our unique individuality
is identical with finding God, and this has to do with the way in
which Jesus of Nazareth dealt with people. He saw every one
of us as an individual. All individuals were so precious to him
that when he spoke or touched them, it was as though a shimmer
of heaven descended upon them. They felt the cocoon begin to
dissolve and something begin to grow in them, something which
gave them the courage to be just as they were, exclusively. People ceased to live from their mothers and fathers. They discovered a power over themselves, next to themselves, and in
themselves that sustained them and that strove toward the stars
and the heavens. This is what it must mean to be born of the
spirit, to be born of God by a virgin. Jesus of Nazareth made it
possible for us to discover that we are unique and individual.
Those who have experienced this say that they exist, not because
they have two parents, but because they live face to face with
God.

The person who was able to communicate this to others must
have been so kind and warm that he animated and awakened
all the forces of life. He must have been so transparent and
clear that he threw no shadows upon people. And he must have
been so supporting and faithful that those he encountered dared
to set out upon new ways.

How do we reconstruct his story in every detail in our own
lives? Are we, as adults, supposed suddenly to step out of the

tracks in which we have been living so long? Psychology, sociology, and biology tell us what we can and must and should do. There is no room to experiment. And then something suddenly begins to live in us. Dreams of new possibilities arise within us. We try to close them out, because they make us afraid. We are ashamed of them, for they seem unreasonable, yes, even immoral. Our feelings of righteousness, decency, and honor resist accepting or adopting or even recognizing these newly born dreams as our own. What do we do in this dilemma, when we must face the fact that in the very middle of our religion, society, and civility, we have failed to become real human beings? We have done everything *right*, but never *lived*. We have agreed with everything we were told from the time we were children, but never experienced our own identity. We struggle to find out what we should do; we attempt to reject these new dreams regardless of what they might lead to; we seek a return to no trouble, no commotion, no uproar. But legends tell us that our dreams are truer than our reason, that the language of the heart is kinder and wiser than the rhetoric of fixed categories, and that the images in our hearts are richer, opener, and more divine than everything that can be ordered, prescribed, and determined. The miracle of Jesus of Nazareth begins when people cease to consider themselves a product of something, a consequence of what their parents did, an outcome of the environment. We are God's creatures, taken from dust and nothingness, but still directly formed and held by the hand of God, and we carry divine truth within us. We have the amazing ability to see God's angel and to follow his call.

In the end, the moment we understand who Jesus is for us, these stories tell us something of the historical Jesus of Nazareth. It is certain that this is how he really *was*, and that this is how his entire beginning really was. It was his inner nature to follow the image of the angel of God, no matter where it led him. He is living proof that legends are more real than all historical information, for only the power within, only the courage of our own heart changes the world and dethrones those who seem so mighty. This is a wonderful dream of freedom. One can oppress people, frighten them, condition them like animals, but one cannot stop them from dreaming of freedom. And that they

dare to realize this dream is the miracle of Jesus of Nazareth.
Only when we speak in the language of dreams and legends,
and when we speak of the messages of angels and of a virgin
birth, do we touch the golden brilliance of his heavenly life upon
earth. Only then do we have the courage to raise ourselves above
this world and glimpse the heaven to which we ourselves are
called.

# Becoming What We Are Meant To Be

*When King David was settled into his palace, and the Lord*
*had given him rest from his enemies on every side, he said to*
*Nathan the prophet, "Here I am living in a house of cedar,*
*while the ark of God dwells in a tent!". . . But that night the*
*Lord spoke to Nathan and said: "Go, tell my servant David,*
*'The Lord of hosts has this to say: . . . It was I who took you*
*from the pasture and from the care of the flock to be com-*
*mander of my people Israel. I have been with you wherever*
*you went, and I have destroyed all your enemies before you.*
*And I will make you famous like the great ones of the earth.*
*I will fix a place for my people Israel; I will plant them so that*
*they may dwell in their place without further disturbance' " (2*
*Sm 7:1-2, 4, 8-10).*

*In the sixth month, the angel Gabriel was sent by God to a*
*town of Galilee called Nazareth, to a virgin betrothed to a*
*man named Joseph, of the house of David, and the virgin's*
*name was Mary. And coming to her, he said, "Hail, favored*
*one! The Lord is with you." But she was greatly troubled at*
*what was said and pondered what sort of greeting this might*
*be. Then the angel said to her, "Do not be afraid, Mary, for*
*you have found favor with God. Behold, you will conceive in*
*your womb and bear a son, and you shall name him Jesus.*
*. . . And behold, Elizabeth, your relative, has also conceived*
*a son in her old age, and this is the sixth month for her who*
*was called barren; for nothing will be impossible for God"*
*(Lk 1:26-31, 36-37).*

How is it possible for God to take form in our lives? We are
almost always inclined to think like King David that we must
prepare a place through our own effort and that we must take
it upon ourselves to build a temple for God to dwell in. If this
were the case, then the destiny of God upon this earth would
literally rest in our hands, and we would be able to decide for

ourselves where God is to be found and where the power of God could become effective.

It does us good to hear God remind David that he is a mere creature and instrument in God's hands. It was God — this invisible, silent, constantly retreating mystery — who drew David out from behind the herds of his father. The invisible hand of God builds the divine, lends form, gives truth, produces beauty, and forges the human countenance.

The people of Israel believed that the angel of God would appear at the end of time, when God would definitively enter into human history. That's why Luke's gospel, which tells us of the inauguration of the time of salvation and redemption, takes up this idea. The angel is sent to the inconspicuous village of Nazareth. The time has come for a royal promise to be fulfilled, for men and women to see the dawn of salvation.

What does it mean for a man or a woman to see the angel? We use the angel image at different times. When someone is saved from sudden danger, we say he or she had a guardian angel. A person who helps and leads others out of a dangerous situation is called an angel. We must think more inwardly about God in order to see the power, which from time immemorial willed us to be; in order to see the wisdom, which would be somehow lacking if we did not exist in this world; and in order to see the artistic force, which wanted us to take on the form we now have. The paradigm in heaven, the model that stands in the background of our being, is the angel. Everything we carry within ourselves of truth, beauty, and the courage to be, lives in this angel. When humans see their angel, they see before them what their whole lives are meant to be; they see what they have been called to become; they see the truth that, no matter how covered-over and denied it may be, lies within and strives to become reality. The appearance of our true angel is always connected with the emerging shape of the being we carry within us but have never actually been able to realize.

We always think that the important and essential things must be done by our own hands, that when something decisive is to occur in our lives, we are the ones who must *do* it. But what if those old scriptural images are true? The issue is not what *we* want and what *we* decide to do, but what grows inside us under the grace-giving eye and the sheltering wing of God; *that* is our truth, and our beauty lies therein. If this is so, then all existence and all being enjoy a much higher status than all that we can make or do. And this is in fact so.

We take ourselves too seriously, convinced that everything depends on us. So the day goes by, the weeks pass, and the years come and go. But who are we really? How much beauty is covered over by all the duties we believe we must perform? How much of the magic of the heart is wasted and lost on all the racing about in our lives? How much is squandered in self-assertion, keeping up, or getting ahead? What we really are grows in the depths. We can't plan it or decide it; it is suddenly simply there.

We can stop right in the middle of the day and make a test. How much do we do as a self-imposed duty, because we don't really *exist* and are not *truly* able to be simply as we are? We say yes when we really mean no and find ourselves caught in false commitments. We say no when we really want to say yes, often out of fear, and find ourselves running away from possibilities we should be striving for. The paths of our lives become more and more difficult, arduous, and confused; more and more, they lead us away from ourselves. But where do we find the still places, the places like Nazareth, where we can simply *be*? Where can we look up and see our angel, who calls upon us to bring something royal into the world, a figure who bears the worthy name of Savior, Yeshua, from the House of David.

There is a divine promise above the head of each and every one of us. Each of us is predestined to carry something distinctive and individual into this world; it is necessary for each one of us to exist or else something would be lacking in God. There is so much within us that we place in question. We mistrust our own potential, and we set everything we can think of against it in order to prove to ourselves how much it is contradicted by everything around us. Our strongest argument against ourselves—the most forceful, the most resigned, and the saddest— is that of Mary's cousin Elizabeth that it is too late, we are too old, there are no more chances, hope is gone, everything is already over.

The proclamation in Nazareth shows that so many years of

unlived life can be given a chance to see the light, that it is possible to raise up and give shape to unheard of and never accepted dreams of life that have often been buried by the dust of decades. It is often precisely there, where we don't *do* anything, that our true being grows; it is there, where we simply *are*, that we hearken to our dreams and follow our truth and the footprints of our angel. And then we become aware of the many miracles lying within us. We need the art of opening our hearts so that the light of heaven can shine in. It is indeed so that the space between the spokes make the wheel, the void between the walls makes the house, and the emptiness in the clay makes the pot. There, where we do not rush in with our own doings and makings but hold ourselves open toward the heavens, there true life begins, a life that comes from God. We can dare to believe and to hope that beauty and truth and life are possible in the presence of God, now and forever.

## Beauty, Respect, and Logic

*In the sixth month, the angel Gabriel was sent by God to a town of Galilee called Nazareth, to a virgin betrothed to a man named Joseph, of the house of David, and the virgin's name was Mary. And coming to her, he said, "Hail, favored one! The Lord is with you." But she was greatly troubled at what was said and pondered what sort of greeting this might be. Then the angel said to her, "Do not be afraid, Mary, for you have found favor with God. Behold, you will conceive in your womb and bear a son, and you shall name him Jesus. He will be great and will be called Son of the Most High, and the Lord God will give him the throne of David his father, and he will rule over the house of Jacob forever, and of his kingdom there will be no end." But Mary said to the angel, "How can this be, since I have no relations with a man?" And the angel said to her in reply, "The holy Spirit will come upon you, and the power of the Most High will overshadow you. Therefore the child to be born will be called holy, the Son of God." Mary said, "Behold, I am the handmaid of the Lord. May it be done to me according to your word." Then the angel departed from her (Lk 1:26-35, 38).*

Some gospel texts, like this one about the annunciation, have to be explained by a woman, because they speak of the salvation of the world by bringing together the oldest pictures of feminine spirituality and poetry from the beginnings of the human race. This gospel seems to say that the world can only be saved when that which men's determination to do, to make, and to produce comes to an end. It seems to tell us that something must come into the world purely from the realm of woman in order for the world to have a chance to live.

For two thousand years the artists of the West have attempted to express this annunciation scene in churches and museums. Such art explores the mystery of how our hearts can be transformed and made more human and capable of feeling the truth of Bethlehem, the beginning of our incarnation. There are three areas that live in the scene of the Madonna and the angel upon the shining golden background.

First of all, there is the belief that this world can be saved by the power of beauty, a truth which is feminine through and through, and precisely therein effective and pure. For what is beauty, apart from the ability to fill something made of matter with joy by giving it life? When the spirit shines in the transfiguration of the body, when the soul becomes visible in the luster of the flesh, when the purity of the heart illuminates all that the eyes perceive, then beauty begins to transform the world. The men and women of old believed that beauty was like the gleam of the sun at dawn, when its rays touch the head and become like hands that bless. Beauty is the crescent of the moon at night, when it grows, according to the rhythm of woman, to the perfect beauty of a silver sheen and its rays spread themselves like hands made of glitter and dew. Beauty is everywhere, where spirit and body meld together, where body comes back to the purity of its origins, and where the essential nature of a thing becomes visible to the senses. For beauty possesses the power to unify our heart and overcome all the opposition between sensuality and ethics, nature and civilization, duty and desire, oppositions and conflicts that again and again cut deep wounds into our lives. Beauty is the power to experience the world as one, undivided, and whole, so that no part of it is experienced as a threat and prohibited, as though it were something beneath human dignity, something that has to be excluded from the incarnation. Beauty is the first and most pure poetry of God. It is above all the art of this world.

That's why the omnipotence of dreams lives in this scene of the gospel, and it possesses a power capable of saving this world. Dreaming begins when people are able to speak to one another with the words of the angel, "Rejoice, you who enjoy God's favor, the lord is with you." Wherever a man or woman experiences another in this way, the dream begins to make this person more human and more real. Dreams have the magic power that can make angels appear. Every single one of us bears within himself or herself a true image by which God formed us and intended us to exist. This image speaks to us in the stillness of the night, in the dreaminess of the day, in the longing of love, in the joy of encounter, in everything that raises us above the forces with which this world tries to pull us down. Everything that lends wings to the soul, everything that illuminates with the light of heaven creates a sphere in which angels appear and dreams begin to speak. It is a world in which we have little faith or trust. We ask ourselves why the world should change only because we sit here, dreaming, and lost within ourselves. Nevertheless, it is in times of dreaming that our soul begins to speak; these are moments in our lives when we can no longer run away from ourselves, evade ourselves, or drug ourselves, but must listen to what is spoken within us in the stillness and in the dialogue of love. In dreams we get a glimpse of the highest form in which God can appear to us without destroying us, that is, in the majestic figure of an angel. When the angel speaks, fear comes to an end. We no longer need to be afraid, for we have found favor with God; we are blessed and protected.

Second, there is an attitude of respect and of a growing forbearance in the annunciation event. There is nothing to be done in the place where angels appear, nothing to plan, nothing to produce. We experience a growing conviction that the world is giving birth to a constant, eternal miracle, and that our life is itself the most miraculous part of it all. It is the respect with which we are able to encounter one another; it is unplanned, unintended, not made up and, for that reason, free and noble and majestic. We are able to say things to each other that enable growth, words that open up fields in which miracles can flourish. We can communicate experiences in which we find the courage to bear the form of divinity growing within us.

What is essential in our life never occurs because we plan for it and hold it in readiness to be called up whenever we wish. The divine enters into our life only when we have the courage to take time to meditate, to dream, and to be patient. Everything beautiful upon this earth lives from these elements and dwells in the medium of beauty, dream, and reverence. And if the hope of Christianity is not dead, then we must admit that it is possible for us to become more human.

Third, the annunciation scene points to the value of the feminine. Male logic is different from female. Will men hear the message of the women in this world?

There are young people who see pictures of Ethiopia or Calcutta or Bombay on television and respond with a simple, child-like desire to help. Male logic has an answer for them. We can only help when we have money, and this is only possible when the economy is in order, and this will only happen once the internal market is strengthened. Therefore, it is not only nec-essary to produce more, but above all, to find consumers. Only when we are good and proper consumers do we increase the national income as a whole, and only then can we actually help. But we can only produce when we get certain raw materials from these countries. And we have the right to do this, because we have the potential to process bauxite, uranium, heavy metals, and so on. And only when our products are finished and we sell them back to these people does the margin of profit make it possible for us to help. This is indeed male logic. It will accept death, hunger, and every form of misery. It asks why it should go as bad for us as for them. We should be rich so that others will also be better off. This is the logic of reality, the reasonable logic.

Then there are children who read that the forests are dying and ask why two million trees must be cut down for Christmas. Again we have a childish idea, a senseless question. The pine tree grows only because it brings in money in that sector of the economy concerned with lumbering. No pine trees at all would exist if they did not in some way bring in money. Therefore, we must cut down the pine trees in order to make money so that there can be pine trees. Therefore, we must cut down *many* pine trees so that many trees may be allowed to grow. Only when we understand this are we able to concern ourselves with the pres-ervation of the forests. We should not think about the animals who have built their nests in those trees; we should not concern ourselves with the entire ecological system established around those trees. No, we are only real environmentalists when we somehow manage to overcome such childish thoughts.

Then there are the dreamers and the idealists who say that we should stop killing other people. But this is also nonsense, nothing but a childish fantasy. Just imagine leveling some impov-erished ghetto and right in the middle building a real house, an expensive mansion, to show the people what order, decency, and humanity really mean. But we couldn't build something like this without protecting it with a fence and armed guards and with warning signs saying that those who cross over will be punished. We have to protect ourselves from thieves, murderers, and criminals. To live in peace, we must learn to wage war. To be humanitarian, we must learn to kill. This is the logic of men. It tries to save the world with male rationality, with principles counter to beauty, dreams, and reverence; it tries to save the world with money, exploitation, and power. We have to choose between these two, between what gives life and what kills.

It is a great miracle when Mary says that it should happen to her as the angel says. This is how salvation began. But it appears to me that we appreciate too little an even greater miracle, namely, that there are people who have similar dreams, dreams in which angels also appear to them in order to protect and shelter the divine. For how can what is truly human live upon the earth unless the logic of kings, leaders, and the powerful changes? The ancient promises are also for them. But will they — and we — dare to realize them? This is the question that has been with us ever since Christmas morning two thousand years ago.

## Accepting One Another in Love

*During those days Mary set out and traveled to the hill country in haste to a town of Judah, where she entered the house of Zechariah and greeted Elizabeth. When Elizabeth heard Mary's greeting, the infant leaped in her womb, and Elizabeth, filled with the holy Spirit, cried out in a loud voice and said, "Most blessed are you among women, and blessed is the fruit of your womb. And how does this happen to me, that the mother of my Lord should come to me? For at the moment the sound of your greeting reached my ears, the infant in my womb leaped for joy. Blessed are you who believed that what was spoken to you by the Lord would be fulfilled" (Lk 1:39-45).*

You can try this experiment yourself. Ask someone to write a story in which the person imagines himself or herself coming into this world from another planet. Such a story would be a pure fantasy and would seem completely fictional, that is, until we read it more carefully. Then we would see that it tells us much more about the person — his or her personality, character, and attitude toward life — than he or she could consciously say. The story is something like a legend or a myth of the person's own birth. Stories of this sort portray the essential nature of the person about whom they are written.

It is a story of this sort that Luke tells when he reports how Mary set out to visit the mother of John the Baptist. The apparently fictional story brings two people together whose lives are essentially connected with each other. One can see here a piece of early Christian theology: John the Baptist and his work are seen as preparing for the coming of Jesus. The early church attempted to draw John's disciples into its own sphere and to build bridges between the two parties, which at that time seemed to be developing parallel to each other. But beyond all historical facts, John the Baptist and Jesus are essentially connected to each other; in an expression of an inward experience of the soul this wonderful legend tells how John joyfully greeted the arrival of Jesus, before, as it were, he himself had even come into the world. Basically, John the Baptist and Jesus embody two completely different ways of solving the problem of human existence. Both agree that the way we are now living is no real human life at all, that everything must change in order to bring God a step nearer, but how should it change?

John, who according to Jesus was the greatest of those born of woman, had tried his utmost to bring order from chaos by appealing to human reason and to good will. When we begin to understand something and want to support it, we almost always try to do so in the same way John the Baptist did. We say how we think things should be, we give instructions, and impart warnings. If necessary, we make reproaches, then begin to threaten, and in the end we may even curse those who do not respond to our call. John tried this entire repertoire of sanctions and reprimands. But what was the result?

John believed that every single individual had to be physically immersed in the Jordan. To put it bluntly, he thought that if all people had their heads washed thoroughly enough, then they would finally, in some way or another, get straightened out. But is this possible? In a certain sense the first pages of the Bible are more correct when they tell that it took a world-wide flood to cleanse the earth of the effects of human sin. Therefore, although it might seem sufficient to baptize individuals, if this approach is raised to a principle, then it would sweep away the entire human race in one great sea of suffering and tears. Seen from the outside, the classifications are simple and obvious: there are good and bad, lazy and industrious, proper and inferior, praiseworthy and reproachable people. We classify actions, attitudes, and finally, people themselves. According to these standards, people are hundreds of miles apart from one another, like the peaks of a mountain range. But if we look carefully, we see that the mountains touch each other in the valleys. And if we look still more deeply, then we begin to understand that the entire mountain range is one massive series of mountains, one huge eruption of earth and stone pushed up by enormous forces in the crust of the earth. Nothing stands divided if we only look deeply enough. Underground, in the depths, we human beings all are connected; it is not possible to distinguish according to morality, social standing, traditional norms, in short, according to our always inadequate but extremely practical divisions and judgments. Indeed, we talk to one another in the style of John the Baptist all day long. We tell our children that they should do this and not do that, we constantly tell them how things should be done, but we know very well that when we go too far in this manner, we no longer further and support their lives, but hinder, suffocate, and finally kill them. As adults we talk to one another in this way, but we know very well that if we continue the community will be destroyed and unity shattered. It is not possible to solve the deep problems of the human heart with methods that work only on the surface.

If we want to understand the words of John the Baptist rightly, then we must hear what he wanted to say, not what he said; that is, we must focus on what he really meant and not what he thought he meant. He who bore the name Johanan, "God is merciful," cannot have meant that the breath of God should be blown directly into the fire so that both garbage and gold would be melted down. John the Baptist himself is in need of the messiah, the savior.

Jesus lived a different principle. He incarnated it, and he wanted us to understand it. There is one single human race; all men and women are bound to each other. God lets the rain fall upon the high and the low, upon the pure and the impure, upon the good and the bad. Jesus did not speak a language of prohibitions, precepts, and regulations; he didn't want this style of talking. Jesus tried to form pictures that were invitations for people to find themselves. There is perhaps nothing more beautiful than for us to come to understand one another so deeply that the unique character of each person takes form in poetic images, in dreamlike pictures. And if we are able to express the unique sensibility of another person in *this* way, then we will occasionally find that this person says he or she has recently dreamed exactly what we describe. The circle between myth and experience closes, and there is no difference between legend and reality, between dreaming and waking. Every man and woman carries within a wonderful melody, a song that has never been heard before, and this is what Jesus wanted to be sung aloud. Let us be done with those people who, following the example of John the Baptist, go after the roots of the trees with ax in hand. Men and women, in their own weakness, their own despair, their own struggle to find ways that are perhaps apart from the path of the herd, need the hands that protectively surround them and hover over them. And for Jesus, the hundredth lamb was always more important than the ninety-nine who never went astray.

One of the most magnificent statements in the Christian Scriptures is the one with which Jesus attempted to defend his mission against all the objections and reproaches of those who were always right, always correct, who always knew better. He says: I have come to the sick, to those who need a healer. I have been sent to the lost children of Abraham. These are amazing words, because whether we admit it or not, we are all in need of God's help. We are capable of seeing that others are suffering much more than causing suffering, that they are victims more than aggressors. In any case, it is possible for us to see each other as people who need understanding rather than condemnation, who need courage in order to be ourselves, and who do *not* need others standing by, saying how things ought to be done.

When the snow goes away the sun draws the flowers and plants out into the light. No fence, no trellis, no artificial procedure can accomplish this, only the power of warmth and light. It is the same with love between people. God knows, this wonderful story of Mary's visit to her cousin Elizabeth is true. The goal of all religions of good will and morality is salvation. The religion of salvation, of course, also needs the formulation of law, so that it does not fall into laziness and idleness. There can be no forgiveness where no guilt is felt. But we human beings, tangled up in a hundred predicaments, need only the power of understanding, of comforting, of patience, and of going toward and accepting one another in a love that knows no end. For this is from God. Only in a love such as this are we near to God. And it is only through the power of love that the new man or woman, who lives and waits within us, can come into the light and be made ready.

# The
# Christmas
# Season

# Christmas

## Seeing with the Eyes of an Angel

*Now there were shepherds in that region living in the fields and keeping the night watch over their flocks. The angel of the Lord appeared to them and the glory of the Lord shone around them. . . . And suddenly there was a multitude of the heavenly host with the angel, praising God and saying:*

*"Glory to God in the highest,*
*and on earth peace to those on whom his favor rests."*
*(Lk 2:8-9, 13-14)*

The miracle of human divinization begins on Christmas day. From this day on, we see humanity with different eyes; and the question is, how we can see with the eyes of an angel, or at least, how we can believe the message of an angel in order to understand what it means that our divine savior was born in a manger? Our savior is born, as the prophet had foretold, in humble and lowly surroundings, where no one would look, far away from the golden glitter of the palaces, outside the throne-rooms of the mighty, in the smallest of the towns of Judah.

The Christian legend is made up of all the essential elements, and it is true. It tells us that our Lord came into the world in the middle of a starless night, in darkness. And this is how it has to be. For otherwise, he could never understand, as he himself put it in all his later preaching, how much the night, darkness, and despair could persecute us. Later, he will pray to his father to forgive us for all that we do in a state of spiritual darkness, unconsciously and always without hope, wanting only what is best and yet being incapable of seeing clearly. Forgive them, he will cry out in that hour when the world darkened, for they know not what they do. He will have compassion for all the hours in which we see no way out and find no answer, for all the moments when we no longer know ourselves and no longer know our way around within our own hearts. There, where we no longer feel and comprehend anything of humanity, in the middle of the night, in the incomprehensible, we are told that God takes on human form and that there is nothing in the wretchedness of humanity to deny, nothing to despise, and nothing to reject.

The Christmas legend tells us that it was cold that night, and this is also right. For otherwise, our savior would not understand the coldness of our hearts; he would not have the compassion that we need in order to set trust, kindness, and gentleness against the loneliness, against the cutting wind, the deprivation of tenderness, and against the freezing up of every kind word. The gentle law of the inconspicuous will prove itself stronger than cutting commands, clashing violence, and the hardening of the heart caused by fear.

The legend tells us, with reference to certain sayings of the prophets, that animals came near to the crib of our savior and gave him a first sign of creaturely sympathy and worldly mercy with the warmth of their breath, as if to say that all things that live are destined to be good, determined by God not to destroy but to show goodness through the warmth of their bodies. It is precisely the language of animals — undistorted, instinctive, brutish reason, as we could call it — that is much more authentic than the cleverness and planning of human beings. We also need this image in order to understand our own lives, since we often enough seem to ourselves like donkeys — overburdened and maltreated, enslaved on account of our stupidity, and driven through life with never-ending hardships. Don't these patient donkeys of life belong among the first by the crib? And are there not enough things in our lives for which we want to curse our oxen-like sluggishness; the mistakes we make not because of bad will, but because of rash judgment, inadequate insight, or error; those mistakes we only learn anything from much too late? Doesn't our animal dumbness belong foremost near the crib, in order to tell us that we are human and are allowed to be so, including all that which human arrogance would repress as bestial and carnal and would try to block out and trample down?

The legend tells us that for God there was no other way into our lives than in the form of a child, in order to give us the courage to perceive precisely the unfinished, the not yet fully shaped, the unripe as the most beautiful image of God. In every single human heart there is a child who has not been allowed to live and who is waiting for the chance to be accepted. All promise rests upon this child, infinitely more than upon the adult, who is everywhere constrained by fear.

We love a child, simply because he or she is there. A child can't do anything on its own, it doesn't own anything, and it isn't a useful and productive member of society. We respond naturally and instinctively to its whimpering, crying, and smiling. If we understand this language of our creatureliness, it surely leads us to kindness. After this Christmas night, there is no infirmity that should stand outside humanity. But rather, we should see a star rising above every human head, shining in the night. In order to do this we only need eyes that are able to glimpse the divine form, its body, its growth, its coming perfection in the middle of human suffering and misery. We need the eyes of angels.

Skeptics will ask if the dream of the shepherds in the night is not to be held suspect and questioned. The message of Christmas is too comforting for them. How can we prove that an angel has spoken, when it vanishes into the sky? How can we prove that we can hear with the ears of an angel and see with the eyes of an angel? Skeptics find irrefutable proofs in external reality; they point out how common, how ugly, how wretched, and how miserable human life is upon the face of the earth. They are right, to the extent that they only see correctly by day, as grownups see; they are right in the language of their logic wherein they can show off with their skepticism and their cutting criticism. But night-time eyes see more clearly, and the dreaming heart sees more truly; for it is only with a heart full of longing that we can hear an angel speak.

What if it is precisely the loneliness of the stars, the distance from God measured in light-years, which brings us all the nearer to this Christmas morning? What if it is only in deepest misery, in the darkest night, and in the coldest hour that the warmth and light of our God appear all the nearer? How are we to trust an angel and follow it to Bethlehem? It says in the gospel that legions of divine heralds withdrew into the heavens and in their place simple shepherds became heralds and their eyes were able to see the Divine One in a stable. This is the message they have been telling us for thousands of years: God is waiting to open every human being's eyes anew; God will do this when those human eyes are able to look upon another person and perceive the divinity lying within. And the shepherds tell us that there is nothing human that deserves to remain unrealized and excluded. They proclaim that there is no difference among people, and no separation between God and humanity exists. They say that endless kindness has come to all beings, and that the realm of what is loved and accepted is not confined to humanity, but extends to all creatures, the lowliest animal as well as what might be considered the most bestial in humanity. From this day on, they tell us, the divine lives in everything and speaks to us as a never-ending word of God.

## To Be Like Children

*So they went in haste and found Mary and Joseph, and the infant lying in the manger. When they saw this, they made known the message that had been told them about this child (Lk 2:16-17).*

On no other day of the year do we experience such a deep longing for peace and security as on Christmas Eve. For on that day our memories go far back into our own childhood, to the time when we experienced peace and security ourselves, or at least hoped for it. Therefore, during the Christmas season we try hard to tell the people near to us how much we love them, and we sincerely ask them also to love us. We need this feeling of serenity and assurance, and we find it only in the hearts of others. Because of this, we make a great effort to be worthy of love. But it is paradoxical; the more expensive our presents are, the more desperately we attempt to reach our goal, the more we fail to grasp the simple truth of this day. And this truth consists in simply giving ourselves the chance to become children once again. Our salvation begins when God comes into the world as a child. And every one of us who takes this child into our heart will later be given the chance to become a child of God. This is the saving miracle of Christmas, that God chooses our hearts as a crib, in order to grow there into a divine form and true humanity.

Basically, there are two things that we need to learn on Christmas day. The first is the healing power of reverence, respect, and awe. We call the birth of Jesus in Bethlehem a divine miracle, and it was. But this miracle can repeat itself in our own lives only when we learn to share the attitude of those who were present in Bethlehem. Ever since that day, the miracle of the virgin birth determines our relations to one another, that is, whenever our salvation is at stake.

To whom does a child who has just been born belong? Of course, we say that the child belongs to its parents. But this wasn't so in Bethlehem, and since then, it hasn't been so anywhere at all. For wherever parents say to their children, "You are our child," they darken the glory of God in this world with their own shadow. Parents are there to attend the miracle of God that takes place through them and which they make possible. But this gives them no right of possession, no property rights, no claim of jurisdiction. Jesus' parents above all others would have had good reason to demand the love of their son. They went through a lot because of him: fear and distress, flight and persecution, mockery and derision, enmity and sadness. But the miracle of Christmas is that we experience for the first time that a child is no one's possession; it belongs to God alone. And if we understand what Jesus later teaches us, we can expect a child to say to its mother and father from the very first day: Whenever you call me *your* child, you prevent me from truly becoming a child. You force me to become an adult too soon. You close up the room in which that which wants to live in me could find its place, and you smother the divine miracle with human concerns.

There is something wonderful about the way in which Mary takes care of her son in Bethlehem. She carries in her heart the vision of an angel, who has revealed to her what the nature of this child really is. But at the moment in which she gives birth to him, she herself stands before the child in wonderment, as if she knows nothing. She is astonished when the shepherds of Bethlehem tell her of *their* experience of the angel. She doesn't answer, she makes no comment, simply takes it into her heart to consider its meaning. The child of God lives in this world because those who could claim him instead give him his freedom and accompany him upon the wonderful path that God alone has opened up for him. For Mary and Joseph this was a way of constantly learning with him, of listening to him; it was a path marked by their renunciation of the typical parental claim to know what was "best" for him. This is how Jesus grew up. And later, when hardly yet a man, he will say to his parents, to these wonderful parents, "Did you not know that I must be about the business of my father?" But to us he will say that unless we become as little children—full of the trust, the courage, and the energy that really lives within us—we will never comprehend how near God is to us.

This is the first thing we can learn from the message of Christmas — to be thankful for the existence of another person in whom God speaks to us and appears before us. Christ, by his example and his words, attempts to show us that we discover in each other the trace of God and learn to be joyful over the being of another person. Whenever we so love another person that we find ourselves thanking God for having created him or her, then we are again immersed in the miracle of the incarnation, the miracle of our own salvation. For it is in this attitude of thankfulness that we will find the child, the undistorted nature of the other person. We will refuse to place conditions upon our acceptance of the other. We will refuse to reject the person if he or she does not fulfill certain requirements. Rather, we will feel and know how much we are bound together and how much that person's being touches our hearts.

Christ will teach us that wherever people meld together in love, God once again comes to dwell in this world among us. When we become like children, we will stop demanding of love what only adults require, namely, competence, perfection, proficiency, wealth, power, accomplishment, distinction, or at least ambition, and finally greed, meanness, and destruction. If Christmas is true, then we will try to let one another live, and the anxious search for shelter in the darkness and the cold will come to an end.

Every single human heart is capable of becoming a crib for the soul of another so that the person may be incarnated there, take on form, and come to life. If we have a friend who is lame, and we ask him to eat with us at the same table, then we will not ask him also to dance. If we have a friend who is mute, we will not require that she give a speech. When our friend is sad, we will not require that he laugh. And when a friend laughs, we will not ask her to cry.

We will return to the miracle of Christmas, to listening to that which is original, not derived. And to be a child will mean that we can give ourselves over to the imprudence of our own feelings. We will no longer need to deny the poetry of love, we will no longer prohibit the miracle of that which God alone brings to pass, and we will no longer reduce the universal ability of the human heart to understand everything to the superficial logic of what can be conceptualized. And wherever adults give up the habit of putting themselves above others and constantly demanding more than people can give, wherever the miracle occurs and a grown-up becomes a child again, then the child of Bethlehem again comes into the world, opens his eyes, and speaks words of kindness, words that give us life. Ever since that day, we have begun to dream of the message of the angel and to see the vision of the stars that guide us through the darkness and the night. There has begun to grow in us the ability to see the hidden greatness of God even in the middle of misery.

God takes form in what is unformed, in order to humble what is great, boasting, and consummate. We are allowed to be as we are, with all our trust, with all our passionate yearning for peace and security, a peace and security that are in God, when God takes on form in the sister or brother who shares the same faith and the same hope we do.

## ꧁The Song of Angels꧂

*Now there were shepherds in that region living in the fields
and keeping the night watch over their flocks. The angel of
the Lord appeared to them and the glory of the Lord shone
around them. . . . And suddenly there was a multitude of the
heavenly host with the angel, praising God and saying:*

*"Glory to God in the highest,
and on earth peace to those on whom his favor rests."
(Lk 2:8-9, 13-14)*

Christmas is a mystery, a truth about every human life, that
only love can teach us to understand. How brightly must our
eyes shine with joy before they can perceive the glory of heaven
shining above us in the darkness of the night, as the shepherds
did upon the fields of Bethlehem? Love alone makes our eyes
shine. And how full of joy must our heart become before it can
hear, in the blowing of the winter winds, how the whole world
sounds like the song of angels? Love alone makes the heart sing.
How much happiness must be in our soul before it is able to
bless the entire world and experience the world as a blessing,
as a place of peace and schooling of the heart? Only love teaches
us to accept life as a gift and to see ourselves as blessed by God.
We possess a wonderful ability. We can take others into our
hearts in such a way that we come into the world again, as in
the very beginning, reborn, so that everything essential and pris-
tine in us is allowed to come to life.

When we exchange gifts on this night, we are saying that we
see and feel ourselves and the other as gifts from heaven, which
we thankfully receive. We come into the world with the almost
insatiable need to hear and to know through the love of another
person that we are wanted and needed. Only then will we have
the courage to risk existence and bravely enter into life. This is
why we look upon the mystery of this holy night as the beginning
of our salvation. For since the days of Adam and Eve, it has not
been obvious to us—to any human being—that we are wanted,

respected, and loved, that with our little, wretched life we are
a gift to this world, a way in which God blesses all of us. Since
the days of Adam and Eve, we each struggle in our own way to
find a justification for our existence. We are not even certain
that we must and should exist, and when all we hear about is
what we must and should do, then all the more do we feel that
our whole life is a burden, a duty that we have to take upon
ourselves like a curse.

The child from Bethlehem will one day tell us that he wanted
to teach the human race how easy life is; he will say that his
burden is light and gentle. But how much must we be taken up
into love, and also into heaven, in order to throw off all the
heaviness of this earth and live in the pure light of grace? We
fall into existence as into a flight without end, without joy, without happiness, without hope, without prospect, always fighting
against the shadow of despair, which grows longer and longer,
and against the darkness. No matter what we do, we will never
extricate ourselves. We can be as industrious as we want, as
successful as possible, but the darkness will come over us.

When we ask people what they live for, the superficial
answers are often pleasure and amusement. But if we persist
and listen carefully, the answer is almost always that a person
lives out of fear of death and a sense of responsibility for the
weakness of others. This is a tormented existence, born in
unhappiness and spawning only sorrow. The mystery of Christmas is that this vicious circle has been broken. At the precise
moment when the day is shortest and the night longest, when
the light threatens to die, we learn that all men and women, and
the human race as a whole, can live beyond the cold and the
loneliness. The light cannot die so long as we carry within ourselves a yearning for love. Even suffering is a reminder of this
truth of our heart. Ever since this longest of nights, this holy
mystery has been growing and developing right through history.
It increases with the life of each person who spreads a little
warmth, who makes the eyes of others a little clearer, their
hearts more open, and their souls more joyful.

The mystery of Christmas teaches us to see in every man and
woman an image and likeness of God, to encounter one another
with the respect the faithful in the Eastern Church have for the

icon, the sacred image, at the entrance to the sanctuary. They kiss and touch the icon as if to remove all dust, soot, and dirt, and to make the purity of its golden background bright and shining with the softness of their hands and lips. All men and women, whether high or low, whether rich or poor, whether blessed by fate or pushed into a corner, are in their very being and development and in the beauty of their person a sacred picture of God. If one looks into their eyes, one looks into the eyes of God. In the breath of their words, one feels something of the breath of God, which blows where it wills everywhere in the world. And from this mystery there comes but one single task, or better, the gift of a new ability. No child should come into this world who does not find people to show him or her the way to heaven, to point out the star above as a sign of hope, a symbol of humanity's true nature and goal.

The Bible tells us that the shepherds were so filled with the light of heaven and the song of angels that they went to Bethlehem — "house of bread" — to worship a child in a humble crib and to tell the woman who bore him their secret. According to this gospel, others must tell the Madonna how beautiful she is and what a miracle she has wrought. May we believe that we all possess the ability to do what she did? We do, but our divided existence suffocates us. We live in a culture and follow its laws. We think we are free, but we are regulated in every detail — how we dress, how we speak, how we present ourselves in public, how we behave. Everything is established according to conventions, traditions, and institutions. Or we escape this system only to become a piece of nature, given over to sickness and death.

Shepherds are people in transition between freedom and order, between dream and wakefulness, between night and the reality of the day. Is it possible for us to live out our dreams in the light of day? Every step of the way from the fields to the town of Bethlehem there will be people telling us that we are wrong, that reality is different, that we should not follow illusions, that we have no solid proof, and that we are only making ourselves look ridiculous. The evidence is clear, the photos are conclusive, the data is certain. There is nothing there but a baby crying in a crib. Stop fooling yourselves. Or is it those people — the ones who always know how things should be — who are fooling themselves? They are the ones without dreams, without vision, without song, without angels, without dancing nights in which the stars shimmer for joy. There are forms of poverty that teach us what it means to be rich. There is an appearance of things that is so small and inconspicuous that we learn to take what is unseen for the truth. And this is how the mystery of Christmas begins. Every narrowness of the heart carries with it the danger that we restrict others. Every dream within us that we do not dare to live out will destroy the dreams in the hearts of others. Every hope that we deny within ourselves will rob others of hope.

It is said that the Word of God came into the concrete reality of a human life on Christmas. But how is it for us? How do we let our hearts be seized by words that are so capable of expressing love that they can rightly portray the being of another person? How do we teach our children to speak a language in which feelings can be truly expressed and evoked? How do we give them eyes to see this earthly world as a symbol, a bridge to the eternal, to see through the walls, to see the true meaning of things, to see a world full of signs, parables, and poetry? And how do we teach them the boldness to communicate the song of joy and thankfulness in their hearts in such a way that it is able to become part of an ever greater harmony? There are unheard, and unheard of, songs in the heart of every man and woman. The angels sang above the fields of Bethlehem. But ever since Christmas, men and women, filled and sustained by God's riches, have been like silent music resounding throughout the world, leading each of us in our endless longing upon the way to heaven and upon the way of the stars. And our infinitely beautiful, infinitely great, eternal soul—this golden butterfly of light—awaits the flowering of the light of love in our hearts. This earth will never be our true home, but it is the path we take to reach the shores of eternity. And we can accompany and help one another in this growing incarnation, in the struggle to become free, in the never-ending poetry of the heart. Ever since Christmas, every man and woman is a living icon, a living shrine waiting to be touched, addressed with the gestures and signs of the love of God. For God chose no other crib than that of our hearts.

## Bethlehem in Our Hearts

*In those days a decree went out from Caesar Augustus that the whole world should be enrolled. This was the first enroll-ment, when Quirinius was governor of Syria. So all went to be enrolled, each to his own town. And Joseph too went up from Galilee from the town of Nazareth to Judea, to the city of David that is called Bethlehem, because he was of the house and family of David, to be enrolled with Mary, his betrothed, who was with child. While they were there, the time came for her to have her child, and she gave birth to her firstborn son. She wrapped him in swaddling clothes and laid him in a manger, because there was no room for them in the inn (Lk 2:1-7).*

Where is Bethlehem? Where is the place where God can be born? It is not merely a city fifteen miles south of Jerusalem, for the gospel of the birth of Jesus does not relate the beginning of his life; it really tells us of the beginning of our own lives as men and women, the story of our incarnation. Therefore, Beth-lehem is wherever men and women are capable of suffering on account of inhumanity and wherever they hunger and thirst for the justice of God. Only in their hearts does God reside. Two thousand years of Christian legend have condensed out of the experience of Bethlehem those conditions and circumstances that describe the miracle of the humanity and kindness of God.

The legend tells us that it was night in Bethlehem. Do you know what the night is? It is when people see, but have no prospect, when their dreams are dead, and emptiness spreads out infinitely, and the world is a yawning abyss in which the hands seek something to hold on to but find nothing, and every morning begins not with the rising sun, but with an eclipse and with darkness. Jesus appears to these men and women of the night as the light that shines in their darkness. It will shine brightly and gloriously upon those who have never known God. Since this night, this promise has been fulfilled.

The legend tells us it was cold. Do you know what it is like when the heart freezes in a blizzard of words, when every step falters upon the veneer of superficiality, and the fingers tremble, frozen blue on the glacier of hardened feelings? Christ will say to these people of the cold that he has come to bring fire upon the earth, and wants nothing else than that it burn!

At that hour Bethlehem was lonely and deserted. Do you know what it's like when children come into the world with no shelter, but only an endless searching and yearning, standing outside the door? These are children who have no parents. They are the offspring of Eve—the banished, the excluded, always with burning sand beneath their feet, always fleeing out of fear, running, exiled and homeless, without rights, without rest, without a place of their own. Christ will say to the men, women, and children of loneliness that birds have their nests and foxes their dens, but the Son of Man has no place to rest his head. But you, he continues, you who are burdened, you who are troubled, who are plagued, come to me, for I will make you free and take you with me into the house of my father.

All who are cold, all who are surrounded by darkness, all who are outcast and homeless will understand the night in Bethlehem, for the child will say to them, Blessed are you, who weep. Full of joy are you, who mourn. And you who are still able to suffer, you are near to the kingdom of God.

Bethlehem on the map lies fifteen miles south of Jerusalem, but the real Jerusalem lies right next to the Bethlehem in our hearts. Another kind of people live in the houses and streets of Jerusalem—the rich, the accomplished, the sleepers, the established, the powerful, the census-takers, the regents, the kings, the war-makers, the violent, the killers of children. The gospel of Mark says that they dwell in the city of murderers. There, one expects and hopes for nothing, for one fears change. There, one clings to what one possesses, to views and ideas one has learned, to professions one has acquired, to positions and honors one has attained. There the people fear change. And the walls of Jerusalem are strong. That's why Christmas begins with the call of the Psalms for the watchmen to blow upon the horn, for the messiah has come. Tear the revelers and the debauched out of their establishments. Turn the busybodies over to well-earned ridicule, for the walls that separate people don't matter anymore. Yes, the walls that have separated high and low, powerful and weak, don't count, for there is no level of humiliation to which God has not bowed.

There was great poverty in Bethlehem. Do you know what poverty is like when the soul is as empty as the mouths of the starving, as empty as the hand of the beggar on the roadside? Just look at the picture of poverty in the faces of women who no longer have the strength to brush the flies out of the eyes of their starving children. See what poverty means when people have to collect old newspapers from the gutters in order to find a place to lie down at night. They are more miserable than animals. But Christ will say to the poor, You are near to God. And woe to you, who are rich!

The child in Bethlehem tells us what must happen for our salvation: we must give up our arrogance, put aside our insane ideas of normality, and gain the courage to believe unconditionally in the passion of the heart, the endlessness of love, and the truth of compassion. Then we will know that we are all children. We were never really allowed to live as children. Each of us was forced in one way or another to get our childhood over with as quickly as possible, so much so that many of us can't even remember our childhood or we don't want to, running away from it as fast as Lot tried to escape from flaming Sodom.

But how would it be if amid the forced pride, the drive to perfection, the constant demand to stand ready with finished products, demonstrable evidence, and unquestionable certainty, amid the mad programs of terror; how would it be if we allowed children to be children? Since that night in Bethlehem it is necessary for us to learn and to practice one art alone; namely, to rediscover the child that existed within us before it was almost killed.

All these pictures and images are right. It may be that the breath full of phrases from the mouths of human beings is colder than the breath from the mouths of the animals around the crib. But we can still practice a humanity that possesses enough fantasy, vision, creative power, and ingenuity to perceive what has never been seen before and to rediscover what has till now been thought impossible. An angel of God stands hidden behind the crib and behind the form of each and every one of us; it is the

pure image of that being we are all called to become, our guide
upon the path to heaven. We can be pushed to the brink of
death and still return from the edge of inhumanity to the deep
truth of an unconditional compassion. It is possible that out of
the coldness of the night arises the clarity and warmth of day.
It is possible that out of loneliness comes the empathy of nearness. It is possible that out of banishment springs a special sensitivity of the soul that gives it the ability to become a home and
shelter for others.

It is true that the forehead of every person we love is like the
sky decorated with a myriad of stars. In the power of love our
poor hands are capable of laying upon this head a crown
adorned with the jewels of the sun and the moon and all the
precious things of the earth, the sea, the sky, and the land. And
so we are able to live in the longing that bears us and in the
promise of what is coming. We have the ability to see the stars
shining in infinite space above the heads of those we love, the
stars from which they have come and to which they want to
return. In every single human being the face of God is waiting
to be liberated and become visible. Will we succeed now, after
Bethlehem? Little child Jesus, do you hear the sound of the
horses hoofs, the weeping of the women in the streets of Bethlehem? Flee, little child Jesus, flee to a far-away land whose
language you do not know. Conceal yourself. Hide in the forest,
hide in the mountains, for the pursuers are waiting for every
word you might say. They are afraid of the truth, for it convicts
them. They tremble before the breath of freedom. It is not a
matter of calling for war against the palace and preaching peace
among the common people. It is not a matter of calling up a
storm, for it can do nothing against the ice. But you, O child of
Bethlehem, will bring what is most frightening to the established
fear of inhumanity. You will come with the force of the warm
southern wind. You will teach men and women to pray for those
who persecute them, and you will even call upon your father to
forgive those who have nailed you to the cross, for they knew
not what they were doing.

Is it true that we don't know what we are doing? My dear
sisters and brothers, those whose eyes are not opened by the
light of the star over Bethlehem, whose eyes, in this night of

coldness, loneliness, banishment, and misery, still do not see —
for them we must fear permanent blindness. The hand of God
will not be able to open their eyes, for God can do nothing more
than be a light in the darkness. But we know what we do; we
have no excuse.

It is still possible to say that we are too little, that we are but
children and cannot stand up against the whole world. But God
will say to us, Look and see how I act. Outer space is so empty
that no high-pressure vacuum on earth could produce a similar
effect. But the dust of suns forms itself out of the subtle matter
on the edge of nothingness. They discharge like exploding ovens
twice, thrice, into the cosmos, and then the stars are formed,
surrounded by planets that are capable of supporting life. Must
we know what we can do? Ever since this night, it is enough to
know that God works on virgin ground, if we only believe in
kindness and hold our hearts ready as the place where God can
grow. For either Bethlehem is in our heart, or there never was
a Bethlehem for us.

## Along the Way to Bethlehem

*When the angels went away from them to heaven, the shep-*
*herds said to one another, "Let us go, then, to Bethlehem and*
*see this thing that has taken place, which the Lord has made*
*known to us." So they went in haste and found Mary and*
*Joseph, and the infant lying in the manger. When they saw*
*this, they made known the message that had been told them*
*about this child (Lk 2:15-17).*

At Christmas the church likes to subdivide the gospel into
different parts so that the different episodes of the one story
become as clear as possible. On Christmas morning, for example,
we follow the shepherds on their way from the fields to Bethlehem. But this is not primarily a spatial and a physical movement; it is most deeply a movement of the soul. To express it
paradoxically, the shepherds would have seen nothing if the
angel had not appeared to them. A child lying in a manger is
not significant without the message of the dream, without the
vision of a world as it should be.

Every single person bears within himself or herself the hope
that the true form of humanity will one day appear in all its
purity and without distortion. Some day children must be
allowed to live as God intended. If a child once came into the
world, in whom the work of God was allowed to live and was
not covered over and pulled down, then there would be peace
on earth. We need the picture of divine protection and of divine
transfiguration in order to know that the infinite glory of the
creator shines in every child who is born into this world. What
we believe about Christ since Christmas, we learn to see in every
single human being. The miracle of Christmas repeats itself, and
should repeat itself, in the attitude and manner we must have
toward one another. And thus it is that no child is born without
receiving the promise of a kingdom of peace, without being
called upon to become a child of God. Children should enter
into a world that accepts them, freely, without question and
without condition, without making acceptance contingent upon

obedience and conformity. In order to do justice to a person, we need the clear-eyed vision of the angels, and we also need ears capable of hearing their song.

But there is another difficulty. We need to go from the vision to reality; we need to let the dream of the night become the knowledge of the day. The second important miracle of Christmas consists in the fact that we are granted this possibility. For as valuable as it is for us to see through the veil of superficial appearances and perceive the secret workings of God in the depth of our earthly reality, it is equally important to be able to recognize the dream in the often miserable facade of the external world. Does this mean that the shepherds, who have the vision of the angel before them, should recognize their own vision in the poverty of the manger and the crib? God comes into this world, the one who was expected is here, and now we must see what only the inner eye can see — that our salvation begins and lives on this earth in the middle of meanness and poverty *and nowhere else*. Without the humility to bow to what appears little and insignificant, precisely because this bears God's image; without the patience to let what is small grow and to cherish modest beginnings, there will be no chance for our savior to take on form in this world. Without the courage to moor our visions to that upon which our senses have been wrecked, we will not come to believe. We have not been promised a kingdom only of dreams, of hoping, and of endlessly waiting for another world, a world still to come. We have been called to return from the world of vision to the real world, which has not changed, and to pick up and collect the glimmers of starlight that glow and become visible in the night of angels, so that we shelter them and bring them together into relation with each other and interpret them, even for those who are most involved.

One would think that Mary and Joseph knew by the appearances of the angels and by their dreams what child it was that they had brought into the world. But in this text it says that *everyone* was astonished over the shepherds' words. This also is a part of faith, that we must be told by the visions of others what is happening within us and what our own way to God is about. What a wonderful statement about the mother of the Lord! We tend to think that raising a child of God brings with it a great burden of responsibility, that everything must be done right, that there is no room for error. The mother of God, however, never *knows* the real nature of her child. She comes to understand it more and more deeply in the course of years. She doesn't just stand there and declare that he has to be a certain way. Rather, she goes with him, and her heart grows step for step with the growing of the divine in him. The gospel tells us that she held all these events in her heart and pondered them. It is like a summons to us to see and hear that which is divine in every human life, that which announces itself and waits upon the moment when it is accepted. And wherever we meet someone and thank God with our whole heart for the fact that this person exists, then we will have taken a step along the way to Bethlehem.

# Travelling with the Shepherds

*All who heard it were amazed by what had been told them by the shepherds. And Mary kept all these things, reflecting on them in her heart. Then the shepherds returned, glorifying and praising God for all they had heard and seen, just as it had been told to them (Lk 2:18-20).*

It is very wise of the church to celebrate a Mass in the early hours between dream and day. We cannot say it is to honor the shepherds, although this Mass bears the name "pastoral" office, but rather, it is an invitation to accompany the shepherds. For it is really a matter of walking at their side from the fields of Bethlehem to the place where the fulfillment of nightly visions and heavenly history occurs. It is necessary to watch over them upon this dangerous journey, which moves from the vision of the heart to seeing with earthly eyes, from the vision of the dream to ascertaining external facts.

At every point along this way from the fields to the stall in Bethlehem people of common sense will tell the shepherds that they are dreamers and seers, that they have no right to lead others into error and cause them confusion with deceptive messages and fantastic, deceitful stories.

What had these shepherds seen?

They saw that the lord of all peoples had come. But the lord of all nations had *already* been proclaimed about ten years earlier; all peoples in the Roman Empire knew exactly whom they had to respect, and whom they had to serve, and to what they had to pay reverence in this world. A *real* leader has money and soldiers. Some fifty years earlier Augustus's predecessor, Julius Caesar, had attacked Europe and brutally killed about a million Gauls and Germans merely to achieve his political ambitions in Rome. The languages of the Gauls and Celts are no longer spoken today, and their fairy tales and dreams are told only in late forms in southern England and northern France. But the language of Caesar is available to anyone who wants to learn Latin. His *Gallic War* is clear and understandable, of exemplary grammatical exactitude, a masterpiece of military reporting and combat narrative.

The work of Caesar had been carried even further at the time when our story takes place in Bethlehem. His successor, Caesar Augustus, was a reasonable man, a true prince of peace. For the first time law and order reigned between the nations of the East and the West. Unity and, we must admit it, peace. *This* is how it is done, how peace has to be organized! What sort of ruler of the world did the shepherds have to tell about? Peace on earth comes when certain people prescribe how men and women are to live together according to the standards of a central authority. We must orient ourselves by the public announcements, the information that we read in newspapers. *That* is the real world. Every fourteen-year-old child today is taught in school that reality is bloody, mean, and harsh. And when this is the way life is, we know what to do. We grab hold of life with both hands and know that we have something true, positive, and reliable. But fantasies and dreams—they're no good. We should let them be, before we end up on the stake or even nailed to a cross. Such adventures never end well. It does no good to hope in their presumptuousness or to believe in their boldness.

And Bethlehem itself. Even the place makes us skeptical. Jerusalem is the city of kings. In Jerusalem there are walls, temples, priests, rulers, traditions, institutions; Jerusalem is well-ordered and established. But Bethlehem? David was anointed king here, that is true. But here too is the fable of the priest-prophet Samuel, who went looking for the coming king of the dispersed people of Israel. He was sent to search among the sons of the house of Jesse. But God said to him that a person looks at appearances, whereas Yahweh looks at the heart. And Samuel had to pass over the stately, grown-up sons of Jesse to choose a small, dirty shepherd boy, David.

Bethlehem appears to be a place where it is possible to see the invisible as though it were real, where it is possible to foresee a great future in a small child, and where it is possible to see in what seems unpretentious that which will truly succeed. Such places don't fit in our world. We are taught not to take our dreams for truth or to believe the heart more than the head. Listen to what the shepherds want to see—a child wrapped in swaddling clothes and laid in a crib. And this they will indeed get to see, for poverty and misery are everywhere. They could go north, south, east, or west and see children in cribs, crying and defecating and whimpering in distress. What sort of salvation is based upon this? Nevertheless, the shepherds persistently and patiently set out from the place of their vision in order to go and see it fulfilled. In this moment they are the most threatened of all people. For if they lose their dream in the face of reality, then everything is lost and there will be no salvation of this world; everything will remain as it is and never change.

When the child of Bethlehem grows up, he will call upon us to learn to see what is great in what is small and unseemly. He will call the poor blessed, because he does not pay attention to external things but only to the passion of the heart. He will see human greatness where society sees only humiliation and disgrace. He will recognize in the middle of the darkness of the human soul the manifestation of light, glory, the message of angels, and the kingdom of God. He will want to convince people that it is precisely in the awareness of despair that hope is to be found. He will begin to convert this world by words of love. He will call into question the very foundations of this world — power, money, and arms. He will tell us that we are more bound to one another inwardly, in the heart, than by the order and power of kings. Within us lies an intuition of our true being. This is what rules us, for it is from God. Within us lies a strong feeling for the truth, and to live according to this will not harm anyone.

But perhaps the most amazing thing of all about this Christmas legend is that we often need the dreams and visions of others in order to see and understand who we are and what we ourselves are meant to be. We read the story of the journey of the shepherds to the crib already knowing about the appearance of the angel to the Virgin Mary. But there was a time when these texts about Bethlehem were considered as Christmas gospels complete in themselves. Only with this in mind can we understand why Mary and Joseph are literally astonished to hear what the shepherds say. One has to take it straightforwardly; simple men come to the Madonna and have to tell her how beautiful she is at the time when she has just given birth to

Jesus. Could it be that we don't know what is most important
at the very time we are doing it, and that we need others to tell
us what it means? The basis for what they say can't be proven.
Seen from the outside, such people never have anything more
to offer than premonitions, visions, and the harmonious song of
angels, a heavenly music in their hearts.

Whom should we believe? Thirty years later people will tell
Mary that she had been mistaken and that she would have been
better off if she had never listened to these ignorant, primitive,
half-civilized shepherds, these dreaming lunatics. On the contrary, she herself was led astray the moment she believed what
they told her. The savior of the world and the son of God, the
child she gave birth to in Bethlehem, is called a teacher of errors,
a heretic, and a servant of Satan. When he drives out demons
and works miracles—and this the people in Jerusalem, the real
experts, the scribes and theologians know very clearly—he does
so in the name of Beelzebub. It is necessary to silence him and
his anarchistic message of love. Of course, it would be much
better if everyone were with God! This man has such dreams!
But what is needed is to make order, to rule people by laws and
norms. We must have prescriptions and regulations and ordi-
nances. This man from Bethlehem is a provocation and must be
put out of action. And as far as Mary is concerned, her son is
given back to her abused, crucified, and covered with blood, a
torn-up piece of flesh. This should be the final refutation of all
dreams, all fantasies, and all the visions of mere shepherds. The
legend in the gospel of Matthew transposes these events into
the past and lets all this happen twenty years earlier, at the
same time as Christmas. It tells the story of the massacre of
children in Bethlehem, putting this persecution at almost the
same time as the birth. Everything happens at once—salvation
and resistance, hope and despair, love and brutality.

But we must choose between the shepherds and the court
theologians, between Bethlehem and Jerusalem, between the
dreams and the facts, between the vision and the so-called reality. The question is, *Can* we still choose? The world in which
we live is a fabric of tightly pulled bands, an inescapable net,
and no one knows how to get out of it without harming self and
others also. We are tangled up so tightly in this net that we can

hardly breathe. Is this what life is, this declared insanity that we call historical reason? Don't we somehow have to escape in order to breathe freely and feel something of heaven? Presumably we must choose to accept as real the simple hope of neediness, the happiness of the night, and the truth of dreams. This entirely different world of God is the true world. That is what the shepherds tell us, and we should protect them with our prayers in this Mass, this pastoral liturgy.

## A Song of Salvation

*For us and for our salvation*
  *he came down from heaven;*
*by the power of the holy Spirit*
  *he was born of the Virgin Mary, and became man.*
                                        *(Nicene Creed)*

The Creed summarizes the mystery of Christmas night in just a few words: "For us . . . he was born of the Virgin Mary, and became man."

During the two thousand years of the history of the church one of the most true, human, and convincing interpretations of these words is that of Franz Schubert. In the year 1828 Schubert was thirty-two years old and already approaching death. He was devout enough, poor enough, unhappy enough, and lonely enough to interpret the message of Christmas in a way that is valid for all men and women and for all time. Cursed by his father, ridiculed by the ladies of Viennese society, mocked by the critics, misunderstood by his friends, Schubert picked up a fatal illness through a careless love affair. He lay upon his death bed, tortured by splitting headaches, terrible pain in his eyes, his entire body one great wound.

What can such a man, on the brink of death, tell us about the salvation of the human race? With trembling hands Schubert wrote his parting song to the world and to life, the Mass in E Minor. Everything begins as usual with the dominance of the chorus, but then, with these very words of the Credo, *"Et incarnatus est pro nobis ex Maria virgine"* ("and he became flesh for us by the Virgin Mary"), something wonderful and new begins. The cello discovers a melody for a solo. It is Schubert's lullaby in 12/8 time that, a little later, is accompanied by a second voice so that a canon ensues, and then, still later, a soprano sings like the voice of an angel, "He has become flesh for us." Schubert, on his death bed, wanted to make the song of the angel above the fields of Bethlehem into an immortal poem to life. If we try to grasp in words what is really only expressible in music, and if we want to formulate conceptually what is set into notes, then we would have to elucidate Schubert's message, his interpretation of the Christmas gospel, in three statements.

*Risk your life.* This is a paradoxical and even grotesque statement coming from a man who, after the one adventure of his youthful life, was swept away by an illness that in his day was not only incurable, but was considered a just condemnation by God, the sign of just punishment. We say that God saved us from the power of sin in this night when God took on human nature. It is certainly true that our lives are filled with mistakes, errors, and guilt, and that we are often brought down by discouragement, despair, and a feeling of powerlessness. But if we look behind the facade of our misdeeds, we usually discover the visage of a child who was never allowed to live its own life. No sooner had we come into the world than we were taught to distinguish between good and bad, to avoid sin, to flee evil, to control our impulses. Even as adults we are like intimidated children, dependent upon the approval of others, mediocre, and weak-minded.

If the message of Christmas has anything at all to say to us, it is that we should be daring enough to take the risk to live out our own truth. There dwells in the heart of each and every one of us a song, music that we alone know how to sing and to play. We *must* attempt to find this music and pass it on to the entire world. But beyond forgiveness of sins, God is prepared to accompany us upon our winding paths, even more than upon the straight ones, and certainly more in times of seeking than in those moments when we have found what we were looking for. And so we can begin once again to be the children that we were never allowed to be, to begin the life that we carry within us as our truth and that too often is buried under a great mass of need and fear and pain. Then we can hear the song of the angels above the fields of Bethlehem as the voice of the longing, the prayer, and the trust of our own heart.

Schubert, a dying man for whom no one gave a penny, left behind an appeal to the faith that there is no guilt upon this earth that cannot be forgiven by God, and that it is our faintheartedness alone which prevents us from becoming as great, as generous, and as human as we are called to be.

*Believe in love.* No sooner have we grown up than we learn to fear love, the one power in our lives that undoubtedly comes from God. We learn to experience it more as guilt and affliction than to risk living it out, so that the step from childhood to adulthood is paid for with a good portion of disillusionment, cynicism, and cruelty. Schubert, who got nothing from this adult world but torment, brutality, and humiliation, dared in his musical legacy to claim that love cannot be denied.

It was no different when Christ was born. We can indict the power that brings God into the world for impurity, we can find it morally suspicious, and we can banish it from the inns of the town. But it is nonetheless so that when we look more closely, we find, despite all appearances to the contrary, a hidden innocence in what we have condemned, a purity that never ends and in which we never dared to believe. And we see that it benefits us to bless and accept love even in its most bizarre forms. It is upon love alone that all the promises rest, only in love does the omnipotence of God have sway, only love has the power to change the world.

We have been taught to accept a weak, suffocated life as normal. We have been taught to live our everyday lives routinely, listlessly, carelessly, without any inspiring ideals, without a single spark of creative fantasy, as if we have to trample down every enthusiasm so that it can't ignite and cause damage. Who are we really afraid of, when we are afraid of ourselves? And who are we avoiding, when again and again we escape into the crowd? Even weak and dying, Schubert proclaimed love in the verses of the Christmas Credo.

*Do not forget beauty.* This is also difficult and shocking in the circumstances of the year 1828. The body of the man lying there reeks offensively; it is hideously bloated, a living putrefaction. This also is flesh, that is, mortality and earthliness. And still there is this saving message, this wonderful faith in the poetry of the heart, the song of the world, the proclamation of the angels, that everything which surrounds us, because it has been created by the invisible hand of God, radiates a beauty that never fades.

Whenever we look closely, we will see even in what is most disfigured the visage of God, even in what seems most debased we will get an idea of the grandeur of the heavens, and even in dissolution we will prepare ourselves for the climb to heaven. We are mere creatures in this world, but ever since Christmas we may, indeed we must, believe that if we really wish to live, God encounters us in every part, in every piece of the surrounding world. They are all road signs to heaven, and we need them in order to find our way.

There are thus three great forces that help us to heal our homesickness and to find the right way to the stars: trust in forgiveness, which makes us capable of risking our lives; faith in love, which teaches us to be generous, strong, and loyal to ourselves and to those near us; and the manifestation of beauty, even on the edge of the abyss. To live these three means to understand a little of what the incarnation of God in this world is all about.

May God accompany us and sustain us in all the hours of our lives, whether they are dark or light; may God make us strong in the power of love; and may God comfort us with the brilliance of beauty, the reflection of angels, even in the shadows of the most gloomy parts of this material reality. May God's love be so strong that it shines through us.

## Where God Lives

*In those days a decree went out from Caesar Augustus that
the whole world should be enrolled. This was the first enroll-
ment, when Quirinius was governor of Syria. So all went to
be enrolled, each to his own town. And Joseph too went up
from Galilee from the town of Nazareth to Judea, to the city
of David that is called Bethlehem, because he was of the house
and family of David, to be enrolled with Mary, his betrothed,
who was with child. While they were there, the time came for
her to have her child, and she gave birth to her firstborn son.
She wrapped him in swaddling clothes and laid him in a
manger, because there was no room for them in the inn (Lk
2:1-7).*

Christmas is not merely the story of the beginning of the life
of Jesus. It is also a summary of all the experiences we ourselves
have had with the life of Jesus. It is the feast and the celebration
of the unlimited mercy, kindness, and love toward everything
and with everything that lives. Essentially, Christmas is the
answer to the question, Where does God live?

The word *God* is always on the lips of priests and theologians.
For them, the word *God* refers to their traditions, their holy
laws, their solemn rites. But despite the fact that God is present
in all these things, the priests and theologians are in danger of
driving people to despair when they lose sight of the need and
suffering of men and women and see only their sacred traditions,
doctrines, and laws.

The word *God* is also heard in the mouths of poets. They
mean the shimmer of moonlight upon the waves of the sea or
the whisper of the winds in the leaves of the trees, and it may
well be that God is in all these things. But poets are in danger
of becoming blind to the misery, the alienation, and the distress
of people around them, and of becoming deaf to the cry for
help.

The word *God* is also heard occasionally from politicians. For
them, *God* means the glorious moments of world history in

which they play a decisive role, or so they suppose. And maybe God really is manifest in such events. But the great men and women of history are in danger of forgetting the little people; far too often they even manipulate them, as if such people were nothing but stepping-stones for them to use in their climb to fame and greatness.

Where does God really dwell?

An old Argentinean guitarist and singer uses the stage name Atahualpa Yupanqui, the name of the last king of the Incas of Peru. The Incan culture was destroyed and their last king was strangled because he refused to accept the Christianity imposed upon him by the Spanish missionaries. An entire room full of gold was not enough to pay his ransom. This Argentinean singer wanted to bring into his songs the pride of an oppressed people and the courage of its last king, who refused to renounce his dignity.

In one of his ballads, Atahualpa Yupanqui recalls how he asked his grandfather: Grandfather, where does God live? Grandfather became sad. He did not answer me. Grandfather died in the fields, without prayer and without faith. The Indios buried him with the reed flute and the tambour. Sometime later I asked, Father, what do you know of God? My father became melancholic. He did not answer me. My father died in the mines, without a doctor and without medicine. The blood of the miners has the same color as the money of the owners. My brother lives in the forests and doesn't even know the tiniest flower. The life of a lumberjack is malaria, snakes, and sweat. Do not go to ask him what he knows of God. So important a person has never passed by his hut. I sing my songs in the streets and when they lock me up, I hear the voice of the people. It sings much more beautifully than I do. There is something on earth more important than God; that no one spits blood anymore, so that others can live in luxury. Does God watch over the poor? Maybe yes. Maybe no. What is certain is that he sits at the table of the rich.

A bitter face is drawn in the song of this Argentinean singer, and it looks like a cry for help for an entire continent. Where does God dwell?

Atahualpa Yupanqui has pointedly formulated his song to challenge Christianity and provoke us Christians. But isn't it possible that Jesus would have sung this same song two thousand years ago, and it is only our distance from him that makes these words sound so foreign and almost atheistic? Where, indeed, does God live for Jesus Christ?

How many men and women are there who become sad and melancholic when one speaks of God? For this word contains all the unfulfilled dreams of kindness and humanity and justice; there is a salty pain and bitter taste because the world is so different from these dreams and there is so much suffering that one can't believe in God. It was precisely for this reason that Jesus tells all those who speak of God with tears in their eyes and sadness in their hearts that, in their very hunger and in their longing, they are near to God.

Jesus was not a priest who performed his duties in the temple. He did not learn about God in the scrolls of the temple archives. Jesus saw God in the eyes of a prostitute, heard God whisper to him from the mouth of a beggar, and felt the hand of God in the trembling fingers of one who was sick. For Jesus, God lived wherever men and women were poor, suffering, and outcast. He wanted people to win back the courage to stand up for their lives against the oppression and condemnation they had been subjected to. He wanted to open up space in which men and women could grow to trust themselves, to grow in love of life so that their hearts would become generous and open and free from all bigotry and narrow-mindedness. Just so did Jesus build bridges between God and the world. This is the way in which he was priest, for he wiped all the fear from the brows of men and women and taught them to find an inner orientation and a meaning in life, to walk straight in this world and reject conformism. Jesus didn't lose sight of God when he looked into the eyes of his brothers and sisters. He saw how they were burdened and hampered on their long way to their heavenly home, and he wanted to accompany them through all the darkness and bewilderment. He wanted to be a brother to them all. And that's why God was his father.

Jesus was not a poet. But he wanted men and women to learn to express their dreams, the condensed figures of their own lives. The stories they told him of their lives, with all the guilt, all the confusion, all the helplessness, formed themselves in his presence into heroic epics with their own greatness, with patterns of courage and bravery that slowly became ever more apparent and clear, and even with a constantly growing appreciation for the worth and dignity of their own lives. It was Jesus' form of poetry to teach men and women that they had songs in their hearts that they had never sung, poems that they had never recited. He taught them that they carried in their hearts an unfinished work of art, which they had to see, to paint, and to work out until it opened itself to the light in their own lives so that each and every one could come to believe in his or her own beauty. This was the poetry that Jesus found in each of us and which he brought forth from our hearts.

Jesus was certainly not a politician. He didn't want the kind of power that lets people do what they want with others. But he did want to put an end to feelings of powerlessness, so that each individual would know how valuable he or she is to the others. The feeling that it is unimportant whether we exist or not, that no one thinks about us when we are there and no one will care when we are gone, should be put out of our minds. He called God an eternal will that wants us to be and to live. What Jesus had in mind was a universal humanity, a kindness without limits, an endless compassion. He thought that because this is what God was like, we humans could also become so. Nothing is more important than our little destiny here upon earth.

Should we say that the whole life of Jesus is one great proof that God does not sit at the table of the rich and powerful? And yes, people *do* still think that God comes into the world in Jerusalem, not in Bethlehem. There is an amicable agreement between throne and altar, between temporal power and the clergy. But this has nothing to do with Jesus Christ. He was never like this. Of course, he also went to the wealthy, to the Pharisees. But the real reason was that he often held them to be more miserable wretches than those whom they trampled upon. There were no boundaries for Jesus, neither high nor low, for he was open to everyone who suffered. Perhaps we should extend this compassion that is found on Christmas night between crib and manger and the nearness of the shepherds. Shouldn't we be prepared to say that there is no barking of a dog, no cry of a bird to which God is indifferent? Doesn't one and the same

force teach us to embrace the whole world, together with everything in it that suffers? Don't all things contain the same force
that runs along the nerves of our bodies, the same sensitivity to
pain that we human beings also feel? Because God dwells wherever there is suffering and need and poverty, we can say that in
a certain sense, God dwells everywhere. Jesus of Nazareth
taught that God's kingdom is without limits.

Years ago a man who couldn't deal with the traditions of the
priests and the prescriptions of the jurists told me the meaning
of the Christmas gospel without even wanting to. He told me
about a time when he was a prisoner of war under the Russians.
Over the months almost half of a small work brigade had died
because of hunger and exhaustion. One afternoon, during hard
labor on the railroad, one of his comrades collapsed and fell to
the ground unconscious. As a Russian guard stabbed the body
lying upon the ground with his bayonet, a woman who had been
watching screamed as if she had been struck herself. Everyone
has a mother! It doesn't matter if one calls God father or
mother. Everyone knows what mercy and compassion in the face
of human suffering mean; wherever this is experienced, a little
of the humanity of our Lord begins to live.

Students once asked a Jewish rabbi, "Master, where does
God dwell?" The rabbi responded, "What do you think?" They
replied, "Does God not live everywhere? Is not the entire world
filled with his glory?" The rabbi shook his head and said, "God
lives where we let him in."

# A Poor Feast

*While they were there, the time came for her to have her child,
and she gave birth to her firstborn son. She wrapped him in
swaddling clothes and laid him in a manger, because there
was no room for them in the inn (Lk 2:6-7).*

Christmas is not an opulent feast. It is a poor commemora-
tion, or in other words, on Christmas we are allowed to be as
poor as we really are. Thousands of years of theological expla-
nations have attempted to make clear to us the meaning and
the truth of Christmas, but we still can't say what it is.

Christmas is a miracle of humanity that takes place in our
hearts and that quickly runs through our fingers the moment we
try to grasp it in conceptual knowledge of God and of human
history. What do we really know about the human history of
Jesus of Nazareth? No antique writer reports his birth. The
important fact in those days was that the Romans occupied Pal-
estine and held it firmly in their power. One of the procurators
tried to raise taxes, and the people, divided as always, didn't
know whether to submit or to rebel. But there was a prophecy
by Micah about the town of Bethlehem, that from Bethlehem a
king would come forth. So what? Not all kings are noteworthy.
The important ones are those who have the power, and they are
not born in Israel. There is not much more to say from the
standpoint of history.

According to theology we know a good deal more. We know
that Jesus was born, that God became flesh when the Second
Person of the Trinity took on human nature, that Jesus re-
deemed sinners by his incarnation and his death, and that he
offered himself for the sins of humanity. These words are so
convincing and clear that they hardly fit into the modest beginnings of Christmas night. They explain everything from the end.
They paint the misery of the manger upon the golden background of a religious picture and immerse the distress of our
existence in the shining light of legend. More pointedly said,
these polished formulas prevent many people today from appre-

ciating Christmas other than as an idyllic celebration consisting of charming customs and old-fashioned practices. How many fathers and mothers today have great difficulty trying to explain to their children what is really going on beneath the onslaught of pious words?

We have to begin again with Christmas and go back to our first lessons in humanity. For this is what it's all about. When the child from Bethlehem grows up, he will tell us that if we do not become as little children, we will never know what power God has in our hearts. Christmas does not celebrate the biographical beginning of the life of Jesus. What we celebrate today is the miracle, valid from that day two thousand years ago till the end of time, that God looks at us in the face of an unfinished child, a human being who is still nothing and for that very reason can become everything, in his poverty and in his hope, in his lowliness and in his grandeur.

What do we really know about human nature? I hear people saying that human beings are degenerate animals who are only now beginning to open the eyes of reason, the most dangerous animal upon this earth, perhaps even a mistake of evolution. And looking at reality, it seems that no view is too cynical. There is no crime, no meanness, no unscrupulousness that human beings are not capable of. Taken as a whole, our misdeeds all lead to one judgment: human beings are primitive, crude, lazy, stupid, pleasure-seeking, and the litany could go on. But Christmas is the incredible miracle that enables us to see ourselves — miserable creatures, exposed to every slander and humiliation — in a different way, because God wants us to see ourselves anew, as God's creatures and as a miracle-in-process upon which the entire blessing and promise of heaven rests.

People may be greedy, egoistic, and vain. But just a short while ago, in the fall of 1989, the people in central Europe, who are normally considered nothing but self-indulgent consumers, declared that open borders were more important than decades of humiliation, imprisonment, and tyranny. What then is human nature? If we intimidate people, they become unsteady and yield to every sort of pressure. But in the very same people lives an awareness of freedom that they will never lose. In the twentieth century we have horrifying examples of what men and women are capable of when they bow to the fist of power and intimidation. But perhaps the true heroes of the Christmas of 1989 are the unknown soldiers in Rumania, who disobeyed orders and let themselves be executed rather than fire upon their countrymen. These soldiers were capable of resisting because of their humanity; they found it better to risk their own lives rather than take the lives of innocent men and women.

So what do we really know about human nature? Show me someone who is stupid or lazy. With care and patience a completely different picture will appear beneath this shell of dirt; namely, the image of a person who has been intimidated since childhood, who has been forbidden to speak and to express his or her own thoughts, and who was robbed of true feelings by the power of fear, by commands, and by the constant pressure to conform to external standards. If we just once give such a person the chance to speak his or her own truth, then we will discover how difficult it is for someone who bears the burden of decades, who has been hindered since childhood, to move at all. If we take some of this burden away, we see that such a person begins to stand up straight. Such people were never lazy, but were tortured to the point of unconsciousness; they were never stupid, but they were made numb to their own truth.

A woman recently told me her story:

> I was never allowed to talk about myself. When I begin to talk about myself, I start to cry, and that can happen in the middle of a celebration or around other people, and then I feel like I'm imposing. So it's better that I bite my tongue and don't say anything or that I say what people want to hear. I just burden people.

When will we let people express their own truth? When will we lessen the burden of existence that others bear, so that they can discover themselves underneath the ice and cold, like the flowers that dare to come forth in the hope that spring will soon come? This is what Jesus must have meant when he said that if we do not become as little children, we will never come to know God. He wanted to bring into this world the wonderful chance to start again from the beginning. He wanted to tell us that none of that should count anymore, none of what has been said about us, none of that which has been established about us, how we were taught to be afraid of ourselves, to suppress our own feelings as if we were wild animals that can only be tamed by chains. On the contrary, God looks at us only out of the eyes of another person. This is the only chance we have to *exist* in the eyes of God.

We hear that Jesus came as the savior of sinners, in order to reconcile sinners with the Father. If we take the solemn tone out of these words and instead of sin use the simple, rough word *suffering*, or if we call sin *despair, resignation, ruin, uncertainty, bewilderment*, then we know what Jesus wanted to do and why he came into this world. He wanted a torrent of mercy and grace to fall upon us and upon our history. He wanted an end to classifying and judging people according to fixed categories that determine who we have to be. We should be allowed to find ourselves no matter what it costs and no matter how difficult and winding the paths might be. So the first thing is to be patient with beginnings. Whenever something great begins, the people who think they know better object to it and try to devalue it and talk it into the ground.

The painter Vincent van Gogh wrote in his diary that

the God of the priests is dead, dead as a mouse. But I love, and so I also live. I don't want to paint God in the cathedrals and churches anymore; I want to paint God in the shining eyes of men and women.

That is the whole meaning of Christmas. We managed to drive Vincent van Gogh to madness, because he saw like no one before him the gleam of the light in the fields of Arles and in the faces of the people, as if the sun itself had touched the earth. People thought him "wild," a painter who broke all the rules and the order of things and changed the way the world looked. But he could embrace the roots of trees, the beauty of the branches, and have compassion for the animals.

Perhaps Christmas is the only time in the entire liturgical year when we can learn something of compassion for our fellow creatures. Every animal, regardless how insignificant, has nerves and is capable of feeling the difference between pain and happiness. There is no limit to how benevolent we can be toward every creature to come from the hand of God. It is much more than just a charming picture to see the ox and the ass standing around the crib. It is a reminder of our own creatureliness, of our own animality, our own need to eat, sleep, be sad, be aware, to dance, to fight, to love, and to die, to give the great song of the world a human form. Our path begins the moment we have the patience and the courage to take each other by the hand and to accompany one another wherever God may lead us.

Only fifteen years ago people held views about such elementary questions as war and peace that were very different from those now gradually beginning to emerge. At that time the American film director Robert Wise made a film about an American soldier who fled from the war in Vietnam. The soldier tells a young girl whom he met in Paris that half the men in his unit thought that all Vietnamese were animals and the other half doped themselves.

Why didn't you go along with it?, asked the girl. The first time I killed a man, he stood right in front of me on a hill, and I was quicker. I'll never forget that. Often I dream about it. I could go to his family and explain everything. But I know that can never be. I don't even know their name, but I know I was right to do what I did.

Neither of them, the deserter, who will be arrested as a criminal for disobeying orders when he returns to America, nor his girlfriend, knows nor can know what will become of them, whether their little bit of love will stand up to the future, whether the power to bind themselves to one another will survive the years of prison. They hardly know who they are. But it is with such people—people who risk their lives, who are unfinished, seeking, and eternally young—that God moves through our history.

We never really know, but if we throw off our fears and have the confidence to go into the night step by step, until the break of day, then we human beings become infinitely great. Christmas tells us that it is possible to hear the voice of an angel and to see its form in the midst of darkness and in the howling of the wind. It is in a manger that the shepherds come to the side of the crib; they come to tell Mary who it is that she has brought into the world, who it is who is lying upon a bed of straw. We have the wonderful ability to see with the eyes of the heart, to see inwardly a truth that, on the outside, is almost brutally oppressed, placed into question, and caricatured as something irresponsible. But when we see as the angels do, then a little bit of heaven comes closer to this earth and a little bit of the kingdom of God breaks into our lives.

Thirty years later, some will question the wisdom of believing ignorant shepherds. A man who goes around opening the eyes of the blind, healing the broken limbs of the lame and the sickness of the outcasts, such a man, the experts will say out of their loyalty to the law, cannot be from God. For he is presumptuous; he turns the world upside-down and takes away its one-track intolerance. If love alone rules, then where is the restricted, confined world of orderly, civilized, proper conventions, verities, institutions, and established procedures? Maybe God is with those who don't know what is right or wrong, but who are trying to find out, and who yearn for hope in the midst of despair and often clearly feel happiness in the midst of tears. Human beings are amazing creatures. In our lowliness we see the eye of God looking back at us. In the mortal husk of our bodies something of God's spirit breathes, and above the head of each and every one of us rests something of the glory of eternity.

Maybe Christmas is not a poor feast after all, for amid its plainness it is infinitely rich. The kindness that poverty teaches us bestows itself upon everyone, and we give the most to those we dare to tell how we feel.

## Speaking the Word

*In the beginning was the Word,*
*and the Word was with God*
*and the Word was God.*
*He was in the beginning with God.*
*All things came to be through him,*
*and without him nothing came to be.*
*What came to be through him was life,*
*and this life was the light of the human race;*
*the light shines in the darkness,*
*and the darkness has not overcome it. . . .*

*And the Word became flesh*
*and made his dwelling among us,*
*and we saw his glory,*
*the glory as of the Father's only Son,*
*full of grace and truth (Jn 1:1-5, 14).*

And the Word became flesh.

This sentence from the prologue of the gospel of John was decisive for the next two thousand years of Christianity. This sentence was the key by which the early church explained herself and gained entrance to the academies and philosophical schools of the ancient world. God is the Word, the *logos*, and the foundation of the world—and thus rational. Therefore his son, Christ, is the incarnated world principle itself, and the person who hears him understands the world and all of human history. Humanity, it was claimed, could understand all truth by means of logical thinking, with the clarity of the intellect; it seemed that the legacy of Greek philosophy had finally come to fulfillment. But this concept, great and important at that time, has proven to be limited and relative. If God communicates with us essentially through the intellect—and this is the proper interpretation of John's "In the beginning was the Word"—then very soon a form of theology arises that reserves God for the educated and learned alone. From that time on, God is no longer the personal partner of our feelings and experience, but the content of lengthy interpretations and more and more complicated doctrines.

How does God speak to us? How do we hear his voice? Two thousand years after John's text was written these questions are still unanswered. Jesus didn't use clear and concise concepts and logical deductions; rather, he transformed language back to its origins in religious experience itself. Many linguists believe that the human species was able to separate itself from the animal realm by the discovery of language tens of thousands or even hundreds of thousands of years ago. Primitive peoples danced ecstatically around a fetish-like object, which they held to be something divine, because it was able to bind together and represent all their feelings. Later they experienced ecstatic sounds, which they babbled to each other during these celebrations, not merely as a memory, but as a repetition of that original scene of happiness and joy that entirely possessed them in body and in soul. If human language arose from such origins, then religious language even today is obliged to make this evident. The word that comes from the mouth of God is able to take hold of us completely. It possesses a magical poetry capable of forming the world before our eyes when we speak it.

Today, only the language of the poets has the power to tear every entity in the world, every living being, every plant, and every animal away from the jaws of the arbitrary and the accidental. When a poet sings of the stones in a stream, of the motion of the clouds, or the dance of the dragonflies, then suddenly everything gains the ability to express itself. Things begin to speak to us. They become undeniable bearers of a spiritual nature, and in the humming and rustling of the world they begin to speak their own divine language. Nothing is simply there, nothing happens blindly; rather, all things are clothed with content and feeling and become the expression of the divine. This is the way in which Jesus of Nazareth spoke to us about God. He spoke of our common life. He spoke of a woman kneading dough to make bread; he told how a woman swept her entire house with a palm broom in order to find one drachma; he spoke of shepherds leading their herds over the mountains. These simple images became pictures of God's care and mercy toward us, and they expressed the significance that we human beings have for God. In Jesus' language there is a holy correspondence between what we feel and what God says to us. And the call of the needy and the language of mercy become an eternal refrain in our lives.

How different is Jesus' way of speaking to us about God — a way of speaking that becomes human, that is incarnated — from the concise formulas and the jargon of theology with which we want to pass on the meaning of Christianity! When does talk about God reach our hearts and awaken our dreams? God is not a concept to be *thought*. He is a person of total sovereignty and freedom; God can never be held fast.

When he stood before the burning bush, Moses asked the Eternal One for his name. What should I say when I go to my people and they ask me, What is your God called? And the Almighty answered, *I Am who I will be*. In other words, no past experience, no matter how cleverly interpreted, tells us anything about the God who begins already today and who tomorrow will be. God is infinitely less to be bound and fixed than any human being. We may know friends for twenty years, and then suddenly they discover themselves anew and become completely different persons. We are stunned. Our human thinking is like following the track of a caravan through the desert sand. It goes straight ahead for hundreds of miles, as if the track were drawn by a ruler, and we think it will go on like this forever. Everything indicates that it will; it "always" has. But just then, the track takes a sharp turn to the right. We could never have foreseen this. But it is the only path that leads to water. This is how God speaks to us. He again and again makes fools out of those who think they know. It is in the clear nights of our dreams that God comes down and touches our soul. And this is how God wants us to speak about God, and how we should talk to one another about ourselves.

Perhaps we at the end of the twentieth century suffer much more from the demise of our ability to speak than from the misunderstandings of politics and from economic inequalities. We are letting the sensitivity of language be destroyed by a deluge of jargon. We are bombarded by a conventional language from early till late, by the language of news reports, a language of information, an ecstatic din that threatens to drown out almost the entire domain of art. This clearly influences our way of dealing with one another. For example, foreigners may say, "I want to make a telephone call." Just where do they think they get the right to tell us they *want* this or they *want* that! We become aggravated. The problem is very simple, of course. They don't know the polite form of address. They speak directly and simply, and we immediately misunderstand them, assuming the request is a rude demand. Even worse, we speak to one another the same way. Everything we say is clear and simple and direct. Apparently we know exactly what we want to say. But it would change the world if we could add at least one or two conditional sentences to ten straightforward assertions. It would give others some room; it would give them a chance to breathe; it would give them a chance to talk to us and to exchange ideas; it would be a language of asking and not of commanding. The gentleness of language depends upon grammar and syntax. How we talk determines whether we reach others or close down all communication.

We are even more inadequate at using language to conjure up pictures, excite dreams, and reflects visions and symbols of the divine. The Greeks tell us of a god who was born in order to heal human beings. The snake is his sign. It is visible today over the entrance of most drugstores. The god Asclepias was born from the god of reason, Apollo, and the goddess of the night, the moonfaced, light and dark Coronas. From the marriage of day and night a god came into the world, a god who was discovered among animals by shepherds and whose greatness and dignity was proclaimed by a voice from heaven at midnight. The parallels of this myth, which originated hundreds of years before our Christmas story, with the legend in the gospels are very close. What the Greeks wanted to say was that a god who comes into the world in this way heals men and women by teaching them to tell their dreams. And that's why the priests of Asclepias asked people to stay in the temple at night and dream and then the next morning to tell the story they had experienced during the night.

When that which is hidden in the deeper layers of the soul emerges into the light, and when we find others to whom we can entrust our dreams as though they were something holy, then we can be healed of many illnesses and protected against all kinds of inner turmoil, both mental and physical. This should not be surprising, for our brain is a product of fifty million years of mammalian evolution, and it carries within it many images and pictures that are much older than the ability to use language. If we wake up an animal every time it begins to dream, after a few days it will go mad, in the way that animals do. We humans live constantly in this madness. We jump up often during sleepless nights, and we are stressed and nervous throughout the day. It seems we don't need the wealth of pictures that come from the realm in which each of us is the poet of his or her life and where each one carries a divine song within. Often, when we begin to understand another person, we find that he or she rewards us by remembering a dream. In these moments something healing happens; in such moments something of God comes into our world.

Recently a woman said to me:

It's so hard, I just don't have the courage to go on anymore. I see exactly how my life should be, but I just can't do it. Whenever I think I finally have some good luck, it goes bad, not because of the people around me, but because of myself, and I just don't understand it.

We agreed to see her situation as a picture. I said to her:

It's as if ever since your childhood, for the last twenty-five or thirty years, you have had to live in chains, in an invisible prison—and this was true—where you couldn't move your body. But you could move about for others, because the chains were invisible. But now the chains are broken and you can begin to stand upon your own feet and use your hands for yourself. Is it really so surprising then that every movement, every step, and every touch is painful? It's as though the blood is beginning to circulate again in limbs that have fallen asleep. Feeling is slowly coming back to them. Every movement is torture.

She then said me:

That's exactly what I dreamed last night! An old woman
stood behind me, and I was sitting in a wheelchair with a
child in my arms. The wheelchair moved very slowly. At a
steep place the wheelchair threatened to roll down the
mountain, and I had to jump up with the child and run
down the slope. The wheelchair was at the bottom, and I
folded it up and gave it back to the old woman.

Her dream describes a life that steps out of the shadows of
others and throws off its burden. And it is like a Christmas
dream about a child who is born again and is saved from the
danger of falling. We can discover our own youth. This is the
kind of miracle God works when the divine speaks to us. But
there is no other language than that which comes from our
mouths. And this means that God has become human, has
become incarnated. And just to make sure we don't stand back
and distance ourselves from the incarnation, let us add that the
message of Christmas could and must be the part of theology
that reminds us that every animal, every living being possesses
its own divine language. We wouldn't brutally use the incarnation of our God to set ourselves above nature if we could hear
how God speaks to us through our elder brothers and sisters.
For it is through them that we become what we are, a part of
life in all its preciousness and endlessness. Again, it is the language of the poets that can show us how everything is holy,
because the breath and the power of life dwells within all things,
and because we have the ability to open our eyes to the light
and our ears to the wind that tells us how all things are alive.
It is a great and marvelous world that God has created, a wonderful world in which God has pitched a tent. And even when
we can only glimpse it vaguely, it is like the new beginning of a
lost paradise, like the return of the banished children of Eve.

# Second Day
# of Christmas

## The Children of God

*"I offer you praise, Father, Lord of heaven and earth, for although you have hidden these things from the wise and the learned you have revealed them to the childlike" (Mt 11:25).*

The world will be saved in the name of children. This is the entire meaning of Christmas.

We do not need to idealize the behavior of children in order to find two qualities in them that are powerful enough to change the world. One is boundless trust, and the other is the ability to take their own immediate feelings as right and decisive.

When we find adults who are able to preserve the attitude typical of children, then we must call them Christians. Children don't have the perseverance that we tend to call faith; namely, the ability to stick to a certain conviction through thick and thin. Children are easily confused by pressures and fears from outside. But, if against all fear, we as adults are somehow able to hold on to our trust and our conviction in the rightness of the feelings that spontaneously well up within us, then a miracle occurs that shapes this earth in the form of salvation. Such people are so sustained and sheltered by God that the whole world around them is able to win back pure kindness and tenderness.

In a certain sense, the child from Bethlehem never grew up. He remained a marvelous child, and he refused from the very beginning to learn certain things that we adults think absolutely necessary. Above all, he refused to learn to classify people according to certain categories even though the adult world insists that a reasonable, decent person must hold these artificial borders to be absolutely necessary and right in the name of God, society, and the church.

Take the boundaries of morality for example. If a person grows up in a "civilized" society, then he or she thinks that the difference between good people and bad people is very important. Jesus refused to make this distinction. He followed the spontaneous feeling of compassion, the immediate need to understand; for him, there was no division between good and bad among people. Like a child, he said that God, his father, let the sun rise every day upon the good and the bad, and let the rain fall upon the righteous and the unjust alike. He was not ashamed to embrace an outcast or a prostitute in front of everyone. It didn't bother him to stay with a tax collector, another kind of outcast. He was so much a child that he wanted the tax collector also to feel like a child of Abraham. Should we call this courage or recklessness? I don't believe Jesus ever thought about it. He taught that the right hand didn't need to know what the left hand was doing, for the good—in the all-embracing, human sense of the word and not in the moral and legalistic sense—was so obvious.

We have also created boundaries between families and between clans; we have devised the iron law of loyalty to one another, the rules of morality within the clan. For Jesus, these were completely unimportant. He or she who does the will of my father, he said, is like a sister, a brother, a relative to me. What binds people together is the love in their hearts and the harmony of their convictions. All the other things that bind us don't count at all—the thinking of a child. Children don't care what woman gave birth to them, but only who is good to them and cares for them. And this is something that is always decided anew. It is not settled once and for all by some document.

There are also national and social boundaries. There are higher classes and lower classes. The way one class acts and dresses is different from the way the class beneath it dresses and acts. Jesus was so much a child that he could only laugh at these distinctions. He said it was not how much one washes the hands before eating, that it was not what one puts into one's mouth that makes a person pure or impure, but what comes from the heart. How a person thinks and feels determines his or her humanity, not the rules and regulations of etiquette, of mere external formality, and not the foolishness of the "decent" people or the vanity of those who must constantly tiptoe about in this world.

Political and national boundaries were so unimportant to Jesus that he could say that an enemy of the people, like the Roman centurion who wanted Jesus to heal his servant, was the only person he had met who really had faith, much more so than anyone in Israel.

The world will be saved in the name of such children, for they love without reservation. They let nothing hinder them in their mercy, in their will to understand. And they refuse to comprehend the way of life of grown-ups. There is much worth mentioning about children that perhaps isn't explicit in the Bible, but nevertheless is present in what is written there. For example, there is the way we deal with the natural world around us. Children are horrified when an animal is tortured or killed. They never understand why it is reasonable and right, and why it is necessary from an economic point of view. They rebel against the order of profit and politics, of business and reason. A child, when he or she thinks about it, can't understand why we have the right to be happy when our prosperity means that millions of people in this world won't even have the chance of reaching five years of age. Yes millions—fifteen million each year! A child won't understand why this is right, reasonable, politically and economically legitimate.

If we continue in this way, we comprehend why the child from Bethlehem does not, as an adult, leave a single stone upon the other, why he immediately becomes a sign that all the people will contradict and reject. For he overturns the public order. He never makes peace with institutions that exist only to calm our fears. He is never satisfied with the well-ordered lies, established hatred, and denial of humanity that are clothed in the law.

Jesus, like many great scientists, is full of curiosity to learn more, constantly to expand his own sensitivity, and never to rest when he comes to a wall or a boundary. But our adult world hates and opposes this limitless kindness and, if possible, eliminates the influence of every grown-up child who has not ceased to think and feel spontaneously and as God wills. For their way bothers us. It shakes the iron order of our world. But we will not and should not be spared this fate if we attempt to live a Christian life at all seriously.

The worst opposition comes from the big children, not the children of God, but the children of humanity, for whom the fear of one another is infinitely more important than the fear of God. People who have been held back in infancy by fear resist and oppose the child from Bethlehem most of all; they are least able to bear fear, and they have to protect themselves by putting up defenses. As Christ and Stephen showed us, there is only one way to calm the big children of this world; namely, we must begin to love those who hate us, pray for those who curse us, and do good to those who persecute us. Our afflicted world consists for the most part of such big children, people who have never dared to think for themselves, because thinking causes fear; people who have never dared to stand up for their own feelings, for they think they first must look and see what others might say; people who have never learned to take their own hearts seriously, because public opinion was always more important. What counts is not how they live and what they feel in their own hearts, but what some leader says, what some authority proclaims. They have no thoughts of their own, no new ideas, and endlessly repeat what they learned in the fifth grade. The terrorism of these big children is the most frightening thing in the world. They claim to know everything, but say stupid things; they hold positions of power and spread terror and fear everywhere, marching about with decorations and uniforms intimidating the world in the name of the one who is the opposite of the child from Bethlehem. They are ready to follow every order, to carry out every absurdity, and to hold every infantile idea for true. How can these children of humanity be saved in the name of the child from Bethlehem? This is the question of the second day of Christmas. Everyone who believes has the ability to answer this question. For Christ has given everyone the power to become a child of God. And wherever anyone crosses over the borders of this world into the infinity of God's love, the world becomes a little warmer, brighter, and wiser.

## Freedom To Reach the Heavens

*"But beware of people, for they will hand you over to courts*
*and scourge you in their synagogues, and you will be led before*
*governors and kings for my sake as a witness before them and*
*the pagans. When they hand you over, do not worry about*
*how you are to speak or what you are to say. You will be given*
*at that moment what you are to say. For it will not be you*
*who speak but the Spirit of your Father speaking through you.*
*Brother will hand over brother to death, and the father his*
*child; children will rise up against parents and have them put*
*to death. You will be hated by all because of my name, but*
*whoever endures to the end will be saved" (Mt 10:17-22).*

What is so dangerous and seditious about faith in Jesus
Christ? Why are his followers persecuted and condemned to
death? Matthew is certainly writing from his own experience
when he puts words into Jesus' mouth describing what in his
own day was already beginning to happen. Those who confess
Christ will share his fate. They will face conflicts in public and
private life—yes, even within the family and the faith itself. Why
is it that the proclamation of love meets hate instead of agreement, that the proclamation of freedom calls forth oppression
rather than finding recognition, that speaking about God produces at first more legalism rather than greater piety? Jesus
himself gave us the answer right at the beginning of his proclamation; he said that what he was saying is like new wine that
cannot be put into old wineskins, for it would make them burst.
And this small parable contains the whole problem. We inwardly
yearn for all that Jesus stands for, for love, for freedom, and as
the background of all this, for God. But we are used to projecting
all these things outside of ourselves, as long as we can, and
setting them against us. Where are these places where we really
let love be? No sooner does it stir within us as a strong feeling
than we contradict it, imprison it, suppress it in every way we
can.

At the end of the twentieth century we have come no further

in matters of love than we were at the end of the nineteenth century, or so it seems. On solemn occasions we sing songs, recite poems, enjoy the exhilaration of a culture that celebrates love, but as soon as the demands of love become serious, for example in our own families, then other interests take center stage. Class egoism, greed for money and influence, intrigues for power—these things always seem to be stronger than that individual passion that we call love. Jesus wanted to take sides for the individual, for his or her needs, for those who are seeking, who are trying to find and know love. This is why Jesus' message is unsettling and dangerous. We can't explain away the words of Matthew here by reminding ourselves that religion and state authority were closely bound together at that time. Anyone whose faith and convictions differed from those of the crowd was immediately considered an enemy of the state and a traitor to the people. That's how it was then, yes, and that's how it still is in many parts of the world today.

But much more is at stake when Jesus speaks of freedom. He wanted to show us that those who stand up before others and claim that they are authorities, that they represent the system, and that they have the truth are betraying their humanity and making true dialogue—the kind Jesus wanted for us—impossible. Jesus wanted us to learn to live our freedom and to believe in it as our most precious possession. To be free means to know and to live our lives in the certainty that there are truths that only exist in us and that we must speak out openly, to know that God wills our being and everything that we have to say from our hearts. This cannot be traded away and cannot be compared with anything else.

Freedom means that we refuse to accept something as true only because others say it or because they told us so when we were children. It means that we follow our own thinking in the same way we follow the feeling of love in our hearts. These two things make us human: love and reason. Jesus believed that they could come together when speaking of God, his father and our father also. And that would make something completely new out of religion. Religion would no longer be a solemn institution, supported from outside, legitimated by tradition, and regulated by rituals; instead, God would be an internal force within us.

This is the end of every kind of external manipulation, the end of every kind of control that others attempt to exercise over our lives; it is the beginning of a *spiritual* existence. It is as if a warm spring wind blows in and melts the frozen bridges of ice over the lakes and rivers. Everything we used to hold on to suddenly becomes mushy, softens and collapses. There is something stronger than force, stronger than commands, and stronger than the apparent omnipotence of fear; the language of intimidation loses its power and we begin to become human when we speak of God. Of course, it may seem terrible to have to live in contradiction with everything and everyone around us. People will ask us if we are really capable of doing this; they will ask how we can justify ourselves when not even our own relatives, our own parents, children, and friends stand by us, and when we have, so to speak, no place to rest or call home. We find the most beautiful and most important assurance in the Christian Scriptures, however. No matter what happens, we don't need to worry, for God's Spirit will speak in us. We are assured that we are God's temple, that our entire life should be free, warm, courageous, reaching up to the heavens.

## Between Laws and Love

*Now Stephen, filled with grace and power, was working great wonders and signs among the people. Certain members of the so-called Synagogue of Freedmen, Cyrenians, and Alexandrians, and people from Cilicia and Asia, came forward and debated with Stephen, but they could not withstand the wisdom and the spirit with which he spoke. . . .*

*When they heard this, they were infuriated, and they ground their teeth at him. But he, filled with the holy Spirit, looked up intently to heaven and saw the glory of God and Jesus standing at the right hand of God, and he said, "Behold, I see the heavens opened and the Son of Man standing at the right hand of God." But they cried out in a loud voice, covered their ears, and rushed upon him together. They threw him out of the city, and began to stone him. The witnesses laid down their cloaks at the feet of a young man named Saul. As they were stoning Stephen, he called out, "Lord Jesus, receive my spirit." Then he fell to his knees and cried out in a loud voice, "Lord, do not hold this sin against them"; and when he said this, he fell asleep (Acts 6:8-10, 7:54-60).*

We just heard about peace and the song of the angels above the fields of Bethlehem, and then one day later we are confronted with a story of persecution, condemnation, destruction of families, of witnessing, and of death. The juxtaposition is shocking. We are tempted to say that Christianity has a strange sense of humor. But everything is in order, provided we take the texts out of their time and understand the words in a non-literal way.

The martyrdom of Stephen, whose feast we celebrate today, was an important turning point for the early church. Historically, Stephen represented a group of Christians in Jerusalem in the first decade after the crucifixion of Jesus. The group consisted of pagans or "Greeks" who had converted to Judaism and very soon came to confess Christ as the Son of God—a confession that met with great resistance from the synagogue. The faith that we express quite normally and take for granted violently tore the early church out of the Jewish religion. The conflict was deadly, at first for those who at the beginning were less strong. But this first martyrdom, including the speech that Luke puts into Stephen's mouth in the seventh chapter of the Acts of the Apostles, is the beginning of Christian anti-Semitism. This speech marks the beginning of the claim that the Jews are guilty for the death of Jesus, that they are the murderers of God, anti-Christ, the instruments of Satan. Jesus' proclamation of love was not even ten years old when these ideas and phrases appeared in the church—and were made an obligatory part of the confession of faith in Jesus. The struggle between Judaism and Christianity has left its mark upon the entire Western world.

Perhaps at the time of Stephen's martyrdom the church still prayed for its persecutors. But soon all those who went to battle against the Jews or the pagans were pardoned of all their sins. Those who killed and destroyed "the enemies of Christ" were holy ones. Life against life. That's the effect that Stephen's speech had, the effect that was historically inevitable.

As far as I can see, there is only one solution to this problem. Take all the oppositions and conflicts that religion creates away from their external circumstances, their historical origins. Then we realize that things that oppose each other for a moment in history are only understood when we interpret them as *internal and essential conflicts*, as problems within each and every human being symbolized in every religion always and everywhere. Then, of course, it is a matter of a conflict and a problem that we must solve again and again; namely, whether we conceive of God essentially as a law-giver, as prescribing rules and regulations that are supposed to govern our lives, or whether we conceive of God as that power and person who, independent of anything we might do, stands by us, affirming us, and willing our being. It's between these two worlds that every person in every religion must make a choice.

Those who want to organize, administer, and lay down a certain form of belief as obligatory, fixed, and certain emphasize the law. They say and think that externals can protect us, like hard shells safeguard mollusks, but they do not understand that human beings cannot bear this kind of armor without eventually suffocating, that this false security robs them of the very element in which they can live. They also fail to see that this sort of security, which operates by means of fear, only increases terror in the end. It is indeed possible to take the fear that comes with human existence out of the soul of a man or woman; it is possible to take away freedom by dissolving personal fear into general regulations and collective constraint. The result is a church that has an immediate answer to every question, an answer that is right, fitting, and calming. We only have to do what we are told, and there is no problem anymore. If only we follow the rules, we can be certain about God and about salvation, But this system of security by means of fear itself consists of nothing except fear; it is hard and fast and deadly. When it speaks of God, it speaks an ideology that carries on destruction by means of terror and fright. How much damage such a church does is only limited by the amount of power it has at its disposal.

Others insist that God speaks inwardly to men and women, directly to the heart, and that God's self-communication to us is through history. According to the story, Stephen had a vision of this kind when he saw the heavens open up and the Son of Man standing on the right side of the throne of God. For him, this is an image of judgment; Jesus himself will judge his enemies. The idea is right. Essentially, when we see God with the eye of the soul, even if only at the moment of death, God lives. There are insights that immediately come to us and that we must live out in freedom.

Between these two things, the celebration of freedom that conquers inner fear by the force of trust, and the establishment of an institutional religion, there must be a fruitful interaction. When they are isolated, they are both harmful.

It must be possible to develop structures from within, structures that can be taken back when life demands it. Such structures could never be absolute, but would be useful for their time. They would take into account and communicate the level of visions, the level upon which the wisdom of the heart is located. On that level men and women would have to be allowed the courage to live their own lives and face the future in their own way. It may well be that conflicts are necessary, conflicts that go very deep and break the bonds between people. It may well be

that parents no longer understand what their children need in
order to become human and free, and that the children can no
longer tell their parents what they need. It may well be that
crises are necessary, even to the breaking point.

But the courage to face conflicts would still exist, even if the
conflicts threaten to bring external destruction, because the
truth is within and the issue is creating humanity. Truth can't
be fixed in a certain formula. We can never possess a doctrine
that is valid once and for all, or have a statement for which we
give up everything and go through the world threatening all
those who don't recite it in the proper way. Some ways of becoming human can be crushed by fear, but we must dare to try, no
matter what it costs. There is no way around becoming a person
and a human being. Fear is only the beginning, the motive to
overcome the chains that bind us.

We no longer know—or need to know—how to explain, how
to prove, how to legitimate what we have learned from Christ
with arguments. When it is necessary, God speaks out of our
hearts—as promised. There is not a lot to learn and to know in
advance, but it is important to accept the moment when it
comes.

On the one hand we have heard that we are allowed to be
like children, we are allowed to begin our lives once again and
become the person God wants us to be. This is the message of
Christmas. What we have to be prepared for, however, is a world
of grown-ups who can't stand it when people begin again, a
world full of those who are always right, who refuse to accept
that men and women want to learn anew. The world is full of
useful, practical people who don't want grace taken all too seriously. The two are like the frozen ice of winter and the warm
winds of the first days of spring. Their meeting makes all the
rivers overflow and breaks down all certainties, but this is how
life begins.

## Facing a Two-Thousand-Year-Old Shadow

*On that day, there broke out a severe persecution of the church
in Jerusalem, and all were scattered throughout the countryside of Judea and Samaria except the apostles. Devout men
buried Stephen and made a loud lament over him (Acts 8:
1-2).*

Pictures and images, even when they conflict with one another, often reveal more than we want to allow into our consciousness. The contrast between the gospel of Christmas and
the story of the martyrdom of Stephen is like the difference
between light and shadow. We are conscious of the usual interpretation of Stephen's story; namely, how it tells us to be stead-
fast in confessing our faith in Christ as the son of God, how we
are sustained in doing this by God's grace, and how we are
placed before God's throne — instructed by the example of the
saints beginning with St. Stephen — to give the world an example
of faith and of witness to God through our confidence, trust,
and faith. Stephen is the martyr par excellence: he becomes a
victim for his faith and witness to Christ; he speaks with divine
wisdom; and in the face of death he is certain of the grace and
favor of God. In a great vision the heavens open up before him
and he sees his Lord and Judge, Jesus Christ, standing to the
right of God, ready to condemn those who persecute him. But
as he falls to the ground, he begs God to have mercy upon those
who are persecuting him. This is our example. This is how courageous and good and clear in our witness and in our readiness
to forgive we Christians are supposed to be.

This is the usual interpretation of this text, and it is also the
only interpretation we *want* to admit into our consciousness. All
the more reason for us to wonder what there might be in this
story that falls as a shadow upon the history of Christianity. It
is precisely the contrast between Christian and Jew that cannot
be overlooked and that forces us today, at the end of the twentieth century, whether we want to or not, to admit the effects
that stories of this kind — and they are among the earliest — have

wrought in history. We Christians appear here as great and
noble; the Jews are portrayed as base and evil. Christ is hardly
born before we hear that the Jews want to murder him, and still
worse, the persecution continues and even escalates. The Jews
not only kill Jesus, but are the relentless murderers of all those
who confess Christ. It cannot have been this way! The Jews were
not guilty of everything, and we Christians were not always innocent, pure, and holy. This is the shadow of our witness to Jesus
of Nazareth, that we exclude and defame the people from which
he came. Even today we have not faced this shadow, this blot
upon Christian history, and that obviously has a lot to do with
the way in which we accept Jesus of Nazareth.

We have to recall this painful episode in our history. The
good news of Jesus, which at that time was hardly ten years old,
was proclaimed in Jerusalem with glowing love and passion by
the group around the deacon Stephen and was expressed in
words that Jewish ears could not accept. A Hellenistic group in
Jerusalem, that is, a group from a Greek-speaking and Greek-
thinking culture, saw in Jesus the messiah of Israel. Further,
they saw him according to Psalm 2 and Psalm 110, as the king
of Israel and the son of God. In Psalm 2 God says, "You are
my son, today I have begotten you." This is a completely myth-
ical text that in Judaism was never taken literally. But in Hellenistic circles it was interpreted as the metaphysical background
for understanding the person of Christ. It is an idea that Jesus
never really shared. We hear very clearly in the gospel that he
does not accept the title of messiah. He doesn't want people to
call him by such titles, and when the rich young man approaches
him with the phrase "good master," he corrects him. Only God
is good, he says. Jesus didn't want us to worship him or divinize
him or put him up into heaven. He wanted to be nothing more
than a way to God, a bridge of humanness for men and women
to cross over and by which they could come to trust in the power
that sustains them. In between there lies a deep chasm that we
constantly try to cover up in dogmatic theology and Christian
doctrine. But Jesus was a Jew, not a Greek, and the translation
of faith in Jesus of Nazareth into the language game of the
Greeks creates an enormous contrast within the Christian Scrip-

tures, a conflict that very soon is played out in terms of life and death.

It is a totally dogmatic claim that is being made in the person of Stephen. If we look deeply into this text, we see that it reflects a stage in the development of doctrine. The divinity of Christ based upon the resurrection on the third day had not yet been established. The way in which the death of Jesus is interpreted in this text is that he was raised into heaven. The dogma of the ascension into heaven is earlier than the dogma of the resurrection. This is why Stephen sees the heavens open up and Jesus standing at the right of the Father. Obviously, such ideas are heresy and blasphemy to Jewish ears, for they are a slap in the face to the entire concern of the Hebrew Scriptures.

The next step in the development of doctrine appears in the fourteenth chapter of the gospel of Mark. There, during the trial of Jesus, the high priest says things that he could never have said historically. He asks Jesus if he is the messiah, the son of the Most High. Jesus' affirmative answer becomes the reason for the sentence of death. In other words, the beliefs of this Hellenistic group in Jerusalem are put back into the story of Jesus. It is the confession of Christ as the son of God that makes the Jews into the murderers of God's son. So for centuries, even up to the present time, a terrible and unacceptable contradiction exists; namely, we confess the truth of Christ, who saved the world, and exclude the Jews as those who legitimated and carried out his execution.

At the end of the twentieth century we can no longer be allowed to teach Christ by condemning others. Even praying that God will forgive them implies that we think about them as beastly murderers. We must expose and clarify this shadow of the Christian faith. Admittedly there are many reasons why Christian doctrine developed as it did, many different factors determining how our theology was formed and crystallized, and how already ten or twenty years after Jesus' death it took on structure and content. It cannot be a matter of wishing that our entire history was other than it is. We have to respect and preserve what we have won from it. But we have to pay the price. There is no way around it.

You may think it strange that the scriptures interpret events so that Stephen is killed and the Jews are pardoned. This is biblically correct. But can giving witness to Jesus Christ be right when it drives others to radical protest of arrogance in Christian teaching? This is not how Jesus wanted us to preach the love that he believed to be universal. But it's even more complicated. Christianity took over ideas from Hellenism, ideas common among these peoples. The Romans, the Greeks, and the Egyptians all believed in a king as the son of God. This was nothing new or unusual. At the time the Christian Scriptures were developed, it was absolutely normal to have such ideas. Christianity took these notions from its cultural surroundings, but added to them the uncompromising confession of God as exclusive and unique in the sense of the Hebrew Scriptures. Thus Christianity put itself squarely in the middle between all parties. In the eyes of the Romans, the early church was nothing but a Jewish sect, not at all important. For the Jews, however, the early church was the scum of paganism. Between these two interpretations belief in Jesus Christ was formed. Because of the pressure from without, a lot of pressure arose within to be right against the whole world. Consequently, there is a lot of self-righteousness, exclusiveness, and resentment in the psychology of Christianity.

All this leaves us with a task that we have to acknowledge and solve. After two thousand years we Christians still haven't found a language that Jesus' own people can understand. How can we preach Jesus Christ to the Jews and to other peoples in such a way that they can understand that God embraces them all and that there are no barriers between us? This is what Jesus wanted. He wanted the Temple to become a house in which all can pray.

Recently I heard a well-known Jew say that Christians preach Judaism for the people, that is, for the pagans; in other words, Christianity is Judaism plus paganism. He said we should go ahead and do that, the Jews have nothing against it. But we must add to his words that we are obliged to bring the faith of the peoples back to Jerusalem. What Isaiah said has to be fulfilled; namely, that we speak kindly to Jerusalem and comfort its people (Is 40). There should no longer be any stones or slanderous words exchanged between Christians and Jews. The price we have to pay for legends such as the martyrdom of Ste-

phen is too high if they obscure our vision and distort Jesus'
message.

There is only one confession of Jesus Christ, and that is in
love. When men and women can say that Jesus is like a bright
light in the middle of the darkness of their despair, then they
can also say, in the words of the early Creed, that Jesus is light
from light. Those who can say that Jesus is the one who carries
them over the abyss, and without him they wouldn't know how
to go on, can also say in the words of the gospel of John that
he is the way, the truth, and the life. And all who can say that
Jesus taught them to have courage to face this passing, painful,
and fearful life can also say that he has overcome death, that
his way is the path of salvation out of this cauldron of fear and
despair, and that he stands on the right side of God and his
mercy is the standard for all times. This language is bound to
experience, and it can be understood by all those who have
shared the experience. It makes no claims to self-righteousness.
It is an invitation to all people. Jesus never wanted anything
other than to proclaim God in a way that attracted all people.
This is the language we must learn, not Stephen's. We need to
speak Jesus' own language of love.

# New Year

## The First Morning of Eternity

*What is time? When I ask myself this question, I know the answer, but when someone asks me what time is, I don't know what to say (St. Augustine).*

Millions of years passed on this planet without the various species of living beings having any sense of time. Before eyes were formed to perceive the light and thus allow a feeling for time to develop—a feeling for the rhythm of day and night, of warmth and cold, of rising and falling, of ebb and flow—there was only the orientation in space.

What is time?

The first answers in human history were given in terms of the diurnal rhythm of the sun and movements of the stars. Time was considered circular and eternal. The Egyptians said it was like a snake that bites itself in the tail. The snake is also a symbol of time because it sheds its skin and regenerates itself again and again, and its coils encircle us like the walls of a prison. Everything comes into being and passes away and returns again. We are merely ephemeral beings upon this eternal wheel. The Hindus said time was like a beautiful woman who gives birth to all things and brings them into the world, but then takes them back again and devours them.

The dragon of time is a monster in whose power we come into being and pass away again, irrevocably. Even before we are born into the world we carry within each cell of our fetal bodies a clock ticking away toward our death; we have inside us not only the program of life but that of death as well. A young man, who was held to be psychotic, had the same nightmare about time night after night. He was bound to a giant clock whose hands turned inexorably hour for hour. His head was fastened to the number twelve in such a way that the nearer the hour hand came, the more it threatened to kill him. With all his strength he tried at the last moment to push the hand from his throat, but he couldn't. He woke up screaming, bathed in sweat. We cannot stop the passing of time, but we can use it.

How can we exist in time, not merely as its products and victims, but in such a way that we can truly live it and form it?

The Egyptians saw time not only as the snake that forms a circle, but also as a contact, a bridge between humanity and the sphere of the eternal. They imagined that their god, who died and always arose again from the dead, had a spine, like an axis connecting earth and heaven. We too carry within our being an axis or an orientation that is not bound to the horizontal plane, but which connects earth and heaven when we stand upright out of the twilight of unconsciousness, when we understand life as empowered by the call from another, eternal world.

It is hard for us to follow this call, for the idea of a circular course of time seems very reassuring. There is nothing new under the sun, as the bitter and at the same time comforting words of Ecclesiastes tell us. Time whirls about in a circle like the wind, like a reeling, ecstatic, South Indian god dancing in a circle of fire, driven by passion, round and round to the rhythm of stamping music. No one knows if this is joy or pain until the dancer collapses from exhaustion. The idea of circular time is comforting, for then there is nothing new. We orient ourselves on what we already know, and the past is also the future. The more our souls—like soft clay—are impressed with the forms of the past, the less we believe that we are capable of leading our own lives and determining our own future. The thought that something really new might happen will make us shudder, for the new is unusual, unfamiliar, not yet tested, not already organized, and not yet certain and comprehended in terms of fixed patterns and blueprints. The new is unsettling and frightening. If there is a future at all, then it has to be planned for, just as all the trains for tomorrow are planned by the railroad timetable to run just as they did yesterday. Only when things are organized in this way can we endure the future, for then it doesn't bring any surprises.

But on the other hand, we humans can't bear time when it becomes monotonous, empty, and just goes on in the same way as before, senselessly. The psalms tell us that a human life lasts seventy years, or maybe eighty, and all it brings us is affliction and worry. We are "like a breath"; our days "like a passing shadow" (Ps 144:4). Teach us, O Lord, the measure of our days, so that we realize how fleeting we are!

It requires the entire power of our faith not to lose ourselves in time, not to let ourselves be crushed into the earth and delivered over to alien laws. But with faith we can take our lives in our own hands, filled with ingenuity, fantasy, and dreams of the new, and do so because we have the power to form the new according to our dreams.

Our humanity depends completely upon whether we live in the circular course of time or on the straight line of a life of freedom, responsibility, and self-determination. Only when we feel ourselves as individuals who exist in our own right, as beings who possess a unique and incomparable personality; only when we begin to comprehend how precious our own distinctive life is; only then will we be able to slough off the heavy bonds of the past. It's as if we were to wake up one morning, rub our eyes, and see the same world anew. We are no longer the past, but we have a past.

We have the power to go through it and begin to understand ourselves from out of what we were, and thus we can bloom out of the lap of time into life. For although we exist as individuals, like tiny traces in the immense expanse of time, we are still sustained by eternity. Just the fact that we exist and live is already something absolutely new in the course of the world, for there is nothing like us. There never has been before, and there never will be again when we are gone. This is exactly why our time is infinitely precious. There is no more beautiful fate than to experience time as a slowly unfolding celebration of joy and of thankfulness to God.

There are two ways of experiencing time. When our heads are empty and our hearts barren, time extends into endless boredom. It is then that we kill time, we murder it, we beat it to

death, yes, we even turn the rod against ourselves, for this kind
of time is a hellish torture that we don't want, but can't escape.
But there is another way of experiencing time. Time can con-
dense into a moment, an instant of incredible intensity, as if the
sun were to stand still, as if the entire world were to come
together into a single second, into a single point full of fervent
happiness. Time then becomes a picture of eternity — everything
stands still and only the present moment exists. It is like a vessel
full of joy, a moment that cancels itself out, a moment in which
heaven comes near to the earth. So there is the nightmare of
time and the heavenly vision of time. There is the abyss of time
and the call to ecstasy.

What should we wish each other on this morning? We
wouldn't yearn for the new if we didn't already carry it within
ourselves as a promise. Everything new, everything other than
what we already know, would be completely strange to us, an
alien appendage. The truly new always and only occurs when
we have sought it all our lives; when we find it, it is our deepest
happiness. Therefore, we wish for one another that there may
be something new in our lives, that we may hold on to the new
into all eternity, and that dreams may ripen into fulfillment and
the fulfillment of the dreams into a promise and the promise
into an always new fulfillment. We wish that time may never
become a circle of waste but a spiral staircase between heaven
and earth.

More than two thousand years ago an unknown people created a wonderful image for the way in which we should deal
with time. Seafarers set out, probably from the Persian Gulf,
the Island of Bahrain, and dared the open sea in their small
boats. They had no other vision before them than the path of
the sun, the band of the equator. They wanted to sail and nav-
igate to the point where sun and earth meet. Without knowing
it, they entered the Indian Ocean and reached the Maldives, a
chain of islands lined up one after the other like on a string.
They landed upon island after island and erected upon each a
temple to the sun. Let us believe and hope and wish for each
other that our lives will be like this, sustained by the daring and
joy of discovery, summoned to go forth into the open sea, into
unknown realms, into new horizons, and to immerse ourselves

in an ocean of light upon the road of the sun. And then every year will be like the discovery of a new island. We will form time in the image of God and in thankfulness for life! Let us pray with St. Augustine,

I call upon you my God, my savior, who created me and have not forgotten me. I call you into my soul, which you, through the yearning that you pour into it, make able to receive you. For before I existed, you were there. But I was not such that I had earned my being through you. And behold, I have been given life by your goodness, which preceded my creation and the matter from which you created me. For you did not need me, nor am I such a great good that you, my Lord and my God, would have any use of me. And still, I should serve and worship you, so that I might be happy through you, who has created me as a being that should experience happiness. Therefore, O Lord and my God, grant us now also peace, for you can give us everything. Give us the peace of serenity, the peace of the Sabbath, the Sabbath without end. For this whole wonderful order of things, which you yourself called "very good," will pass away, when it has fulfilled the measure set for it. Then it will have had its morning and its evening. The seventh day, however, has no evening and thus no end, for you have made it holy, so that it may last forever. Then you will rest in us just as now you work in us, and so will that peace be your peace in us like our works here below are your works through us. You, however, Lord, are always at work and always at rest. You do not see time, nor move in time, nor rest in time, and still you make knowledge, time itself, and the rest at the end of time (*Confessions*).

My dear sisters and brothers, this is what we want to wish one another, to rest in God in the middle of time and, no matter what we do, to do it in the power of God's hands. We want to carry in our hearts the peace of happiness, just as on the last morning of creation and the first morning of eternity.

## The World of Tomorrow

*"But he who acts in truth*
*comes into the light,*
*to make clear*
*that his deeds are done in God" (Jn 3:21).*

Christianity understands itself as a religion that marks a turning point in history. The Christian faith marks the hope in a new world, a world that changes everything that once was, even overcomes sin and frees us from its power.

But what is actually new in our lives when we come to believe in Christ? The information we receive in the catechism or in the history books is not new, for what is new cannot be found upon the level of facts. It is best discovered through a change in our attitude and in the way we live, for it is out of these that deeds and facts arise. According to the newspapers there will be nothing new in the new year. Not even a new life being born into the world is new in the eyes of the statisticians. They tell us that the human race as a whole will continue to increase. People will come and go. The problem of overpopulation will remain. Wars and earthquakes will continue to occur. But there will also be negotiations, peace treaties, and new discoveries in the fight against disease. We fear some of these things and hope for others. But our *real* hope is that nothing changes, for this would be too disturbing.

Nevertheless, we are perhaps the first generation that also feels things *can't* go on as they have. We feel that everything that we have heretofore called history must be written anew. We are certainly the first human beings upon this planet with a fairly correct feeling for the immense magnitude of time. It has only been within the last hundred years that we have begun to accept the fact that the earth has existed for about five billion years and that higher forms of life have existed upon it for almost seven hundred million years. Comparing these figures to the span of what we usually call history gives us a clear picture of what time really means.

At the moment there is nothing we fear more than a nuclear war. We contemplate the effects of global radioactive pollution with horror. The fallout from uranium fission bombs in the form of Strontium 90 has a half-life of 28,000 years — about four times longer than the entire span of time we call civilized history! No one can imagine human progress in terms of such immense tracts of time. But in the realm of nature, in the history of the earth, these years are a tiny moment. How many times must we multiply thirty thousand in order to get a million? Even the estimates for the appearance of our own species belong within the bounds of, say two, three, or four million years.

The biography of homo sapiens simply disappears in the immense intervals of geological history. The magnitude of it all is unimaginable. Nevertheless, in the bosom of the ages, our soul, our body, and also what we call the laws of history have been formed, and this increasingly causes us problems and suffering today. Everything that has made us great in the past can destroy us tomorrow, if we don't change it. Today we know more clearly than ever that we are not allowed to use our highly complex thirteen million brain cells and all the means that advanced technology places at our disposal to devour ourselves and our environment.

What has human society been up till now? How have we ordered our communal life? We have two instincts in us of archaic power and force, so strong that in comparison to them individual consciousness appears like a frail toy tossed upon the surging waters. These are aggression and sexuality.

Aggression has meant that up till now every human group is based, in one way or another, upon the struggle for power. The person who is best able to assert himself or herself will have the say within the group. We have accepted this as settled, as fully normal, and as absolutely necessary. Even today we believe that we can accept this and at the same time be capable of living together peacefully. But wherever human community is constituted by the attainment of power and by the ability to establish strength, the consequences are war, conquest, and oppression inside and outside the group. This is absolutely unavoidable. To say it clearly, as long as we conduct politics as the institutionalization and organization of this way of building community, as the administration and enforcement of mass egoism, as the art of winning, maintaining, and extending power, we will never really read anything new in the newspapers. We will again and again be confronted with the same old nightmares happening at different places on earth with ever-increasing numbers of casualties and victims. There will indeed be nothing new under the sun.

Jesus tells his disciples, as though it were obvious, that the person who wants to be great should be the servant of all. He says that while the mighty let themselves be called benefactors, we should not do this. We would be wise to take such simple statements from the Christian Scriptures as programs for survival. We will not become people who are truly capable of living upon this earth unless we stop asking ourselves how we can best conquer and rule over others, over our surroundings, and over those who are near to us; instead, we must begin to ask how we can try to find out what other people really need, what will truly help them, what is actually useful to them, and how we can give them what they need. This is a genuinely new way of thinking. The new model of human nature is not the roaring gorilla, but people who are able to listen to the needs of others and who can become sensitive enough to hear and "obey" one another.

The human ability to use reason against nature and to wage war upon the earth in order to exploit and make use of its natural resources is also associated with the instinct of aggression. This too will have to change. Human beings should not be defined by their ability to make money by robbing natural treasures and by processing natural resources for the purpose of gaining a profit on the market, a profit that then flows into their own pocketbook. Still less should a civilization be judged by how much energy it can consume.

Perhaps we can learn a lot more about humanity from the so-called social problems. For example, we are learning from the millions of unemployed that the growth of the various social services is probably a good standard by which to measure a higher civilization. Maybe we will learn one day that the development of our human nature lies in the voluntary, unpaid, and unaccounted for services that a society is able to provide to its members free of all pride and struggle for the attainment of power. On the whole, our thinking and planning has been oriented to what can be done and must be done. But our future way of life may be what I call "impressionistic." In this future we will be capable of accepting instead of wanting to change everything, capable of understanding instead of grabbing and possessing. In this future we will develop a poetry and creativity in dealing with ourselves and with the world around us.

Let's take an example. Most of our time is spent between obligatory work and time-off relaxation. But what in our lives do we do because we want to, and what do we do simply to avoid boredom? A poet, we could say, is someone who is never bored. Throw a poet into the filthiest of prison cells, and he or she will begin to describe it in detail. How many of all the things that we have seen today could we describe with a paintbrush, a pencil, or a pen, making poetry, music, or art out of it? A human face, a landscape, the words of a conversation—what of all this could we transcribe in such a way that it would be relatively accurate and communicate a real experience that we have had? The ability to see things in terms of their beauty and their deep structure, not merely in terms of their usefulness, may well be a form of survival or even the way we can enter into a genuine and authentic life.

We are told that the second great instinct, sexuality, has also deeply conditioned us. It has long been associated only with the will to preserve the species, to bear children, and to hand on the genetic material of the race. Marriage was a contractual exchange of property; people belonged to each other like possessions, all in accordance with the ten commandments, which tell us we ought not to covet our neighbor's wife, or his ox, or his mule, or anything else that belongs to him. This way of thinking has led us into a terrible crisis. The immense increase in population is breaking upon the already too narrow walls of nature like a tidal wave; indeed, the flood is already flowing back at us with an enormous deluge of deaths, of hunger, and misery. We must try to imagine and discover new forms of interacting with each other on the basis of the sexual instinct. We must learn to use our wonderful sexual energy to invent and to practice forms of friendship that are open, free, and unconstrained by external interests and purposes; to discover new forms of sensibility, of receptiveness, of responsiveness; and to create a true poetry of human relations. This would not be a possessive sexuality, but a sexuality based upon the feelings of the heart, which let the partners experience life much more openly and intensively than ever before.

We consider sexual energy as something we must simply work off. But what if it is really an energy that flows through every day and every moment of our lives? Again, it is the poets, the musicians, and the painters who experience the world in an erotic rapture and vitality. I see no other way to live a truly human life than to learn to listen to the wonderful music of this world, to hear the beauty of its harmonious singing, to follow its subtle movements, and to discover a completely new feeling for its unity.

The best way to become human will consist in praying more deeply, worshipping with a more generous and open heart, and on the whole, being more devout, more thankful, and more sensitive. In the world of tomorrow we, as individuals, will be needed more than ever. For many millions of years nature has been striving to produce ever more complicated organisms. We are not standing at the end of our history. Each of us can learn things that are only accessible to us as individuals, things that are ever more rich and beautiful. And we will need one another, each to contribute his or her own unique knowledge and creativity. Then we will be able to expect and hope for that absolutely new event that opens out onto eternity.

Time consists in separating what comes before from what comes after. But even today there are moments of happiness and bliss in which everything we hope for and everything we can remember come together in a single instant. If we imagine this instant as an eternal present, a moment that stands still, an instant that never passes, but contains within it the unity of all men and women, the harmony of the entire universe, the condensed experience of each and every one of us in the communion of love, then we have perhaps a vague idea of what that absolutely new event that is awaiting us in God might be.

## Finding Our Name

*Then the shepherds returned, glorifying and praising God for
all they had heard and seen, just as it had been told to them.
When eight days were completed for his circumcision, he was
named Jesus, the name given him by the angel before he was
conceived in the womb (Lk 2:20-21).*

Everywhere in the world people practice the old custom of
taking a newborn infant to the temple or church in order to
dedicate it to God and to the sphere of the divine. There is deep
wisdom in this custom, for at this time of great helplessness a
child appears to belong completely to its parents. This is also
the time parents are most thankful for the gift they have
received; they not only feel responsible for the newborn infant,
but also see in it the fulfillment, yes, even the entire meaning
of their own lives. It is therefore painful, but nevertheless right
and necessary, that precisely at this time almost all religions
require parents to dedicate their children to an unseen power,
a power to which we owe our being and whose instruments we
are, even as fathers and mothers. We are never the masters of
life, but only its servants.

No one belongs to another person, but only to God. In Christianity we express this very beautifully when we bring a child
into the church in order to give it its true name. This "second
birth" makes a child who has come into the world by natural
parents into a child of God. We are saying that only God knows
who we truly are and that only God can know our real name.
Basically, this is also what the legend about the child Jesus being
brought to the Temple in Jerusalem says. And it is valid for
every human being. We find our name in the temple or church
itself, that is, in the holy place. We also learn there to say this
name, so that it is valid for our whole life. That's why myths and
legends all over the world say that the announcement of such a
holy name is a special event that occurs in dreams, or as the
message of an angel, or in revelations of all sorts. They tell us
that it is an art to hear and to understand the name of a person.

How do we hear the message of an angel telling us the name of another person? Today we live in a culture that is still very much influenced by ancient Rome. The Romans were a practical people, and they named their children just as they came, numbered from one to ten, *Primus, Secundus,* . . . *Decimus* — names with no illusions. No one could claim that a certain name embodied something essential, for a name signified the place one had in the series of births and nothing else. The names we give our children today often come from the world of glamour and celebrity. The children represent their parent's hopes for success, for beauty, and for influence, and perhaps their names are meant to embody a little of the fame and glory of an illusory heaven, a heaven made up of the glittering lights that appear on the stages of this world. If this were all there was to it, our children would be destined, as soon as they saw the light of day, to vanish into an imaginary world of excitement and activity.

But there is more to it. It's important for us to remember that there is a place reserved for God and for the experiences of our dreams, a place to know what our real name is. It's like a memory of the beginnings of the human race, when Adam in paradise fell into a deep sleep and dreamed with all the longing of love of another person whom he had to encounter in order to make his life full and happy. Only when he awoke and saw the partner he loved did he give her a name. And so it is with us.

Out of the dreaming poetry of love we make up affectionate names for each other, names so intimate and private that they can never be spoken in public, names that attempt to find that one true name that God has given us and that we often cannot find or know as long as we live. Love can be so strong that it speaks the name of the beloved in a way that changes the world, like a magical spell, and creates a secret center to which all paths lead. We find that we must recite such a name like a neverending litany, like something that is holy in itself, like a word of blessing. For it is in the name of love that we begin to give names to everything around us in a different way and thus truly to understand what things are.

Much with which we concern ourselves otherwise is so accidental, so arbitrary, so much merely something that could just as well not be, that we wouldn't miss it if it were not there; it is not essential. It is love alone that leads us to the point where we can say that this one person, together with the whole concert of stars and the entire cosmos, *must* exist, for without all this, this one person with his or her unique name would not exist either. Love leads us to the point where we begin to understand everything. We begin to comprehend the power to which we owe everything we have and the force that makes the world around us and the place in which we live into a holy space, a sanctuary that will never perish.

Perhaps it is the Eastern church that best understands the celebration of the name of Jesus. It has developed a form of prayer that consists in constantly repeating the name of Jesus from out of the depths of the heart, of repeating this holy name until exhaustion, until it becomes a song within the heart that never ceases binding us to the whole world. This is a belief in Christ as the place where we most deeply and clearly are able to understand who God is and who we ourselves can become. It is the end of fear, the beginning of hope, and the basis of our true dignity and worth. That's why Jesus is the savior from fear, from alienation, from humiliation, and from degradation; that's why he is a shining light in the middle of the darkness of this world. Jesus, the savior, is his name—just as the angel said when he was conceived by the holy Spirit of the Virgin Mary. Even before we are born, God has a plan for us, an idea of who we are to become. This is the theme of our life, the task we are given to complete in this life.

Now, at the beginning of the new year, let us ask ourselves what is so new about the fact that the clock has struck twelve once again. Nothing is really new. But it would be something wonderful, if we could enter deeply into the mystery of the life of another person. There, we will find much that is new, much that is already known, much that is great, and much that has never been seen and is waiting to be discovered. And the more we are able to do this, the more will the world change and renew itself and bloom like a flower at dawn.

# First Sunday
# after Christmas

## Listening to the Night

*When they had departed, behold, the angel of the Lord appeared to Joseph in a dream and said, "Rise, take the child and his mother, flee to Egypt, and stay there until I tell you. Herod is going to search for the child to destroy him." Joseph rose and took the child and his mother by night and departed for Egypt. He stayed there until the death of Herod, that what the Lord had said through the prophet might be fulfilled, "Out of Egypt I called my son."*

*When Herod realized that he had been deceived by the magi, he became furious. He ordered the massacre of all the boys in Bethlehem and its vicinity two years old and under, in accordance with the time he had ascertained from the magi. Then was fulfilled what had been said through Jeremiah the prophet:*

> *"A voice was heard in Ramah,*
> *sobbing and loud lamentation;*
> *Rachel weeping for her children,*
> *and she would not be consoled,*
> *since they were no more."*

*When Herod had died, behold, the angel of the Lord appeared in a dream to Joseph in Egypt and said, "Rise, take the child and his mother and go to the land of Israel, for those who sought the child's life are dead." He rose, took the child and his mother, and went to the land of Israel. But when he*

*heard that Archelaus was ruling over Judea in place of his*
*father Herod, he was afraid to go back there. And because he*
*had been warned in a dream, he departed for the region of*
*Galilee. He went and dwelt in a town called Nazareth, so that*
*what had been spoken through the prophets might be fulfilled,*
*"He shall be called a Nazorean" (Mt 2:13-23).*

Matthew continues the story of the birth of our savior as a
chain of fulfilled prophecies. But it is so surprising, so full of
contradictions, so upsetting, and so contrary to our expectations
that it almost takes our breath away. The human race had waited
for centuries, even for millennia for the arrival of the savior,
and when he finally comes peace does not spread across the face
of the earth like a gentle rain from heaven. On the contrary, it
seems that all the dark sources of violence and hatred must first
come out into the open before the earth can bear the fruits of
peace.

We can see why Matthew places the saying of the prophet,
"I have called my son out of Egypt," at the beginning of the
story. For the entire destiny of the chosen people is condensed
into the destiny of Jesus. We understand this immediately, and
this is how it must be. If we are to experience any kind of liberation and salvation today, then it must be as it was for Israel
when it was freed from the domination of the pharaohs and led
out of Egypt into freedom. This liberation does not occur without fear and hardship, without struggle and determination, but
still it leads to the place we are destined to be, to a promised
land. The destiny of all of Israel is represented and repeated in
the person of Jesus — thus the flight in the night, the banishment
into Egypt, and the return to the homeland. Matthew intends
this to be understood as fulfilled prophecy.

The prophecy of Isaiah is also represented in Jesus. There it
is said that our salvation will shoot forth from the stem of Jesse,
and at the time of judgment Israel will be chosen as the secret
middle point of the world and all peoples will look to her. Then
it will happen that the kings of the islands and from all the ends
of the earth, from the kingdoms of Sheba and beyond the desert,
will come to Sinai, to the place from which light will fall upon
all those who are in darkness. This is what we hope for.

But it is terrible that the dark words of Jeremiah are placed
like a trumpet blast in the middle of the proclamation of hope
we hear at Christmas. For Jeremiah, the sobbing and weeping
of Rachel was not prophecy; it was taking place before his very
eyes. In his mind's eye he saw Rachel, the ancestral mother of
Israel, upon the heights of Ramah, weeping and lamenting for
her children, who were being deported into exile under the whip
of the Babylonians. Will this spirit of violence, of ever-recurring
destruction for the sake of dominating and enslaving others ever
come to an end? Or will it continue, each time more devastating
than before? This is what Matthew is thinking. He is well-aware
of these questions, at least since the death of Jesus.

We do not immediately and clearly understand that which we
most yearn for. After thousands of years of waiting we are not
able to greet and acclaim our own freedom when it finally comes.
On the contrary, there is nothing we are more afraid of than a
life free from fear, a life exposed to the openness of our own
possibilities. We are afraid to lose all the things we have clung
to for security. We are repelled by the thought of an existence
apparently so unprotected that it is based only upon the invisible
presence of God. The whole world seems to fall apart precisely
at the moment of salvation. And this is how the myths of all
peoples everywhere and at all times—not just Matthew's gospel—have described it. No sooner is the savior born than a
tyrannical ruler arises who plots to destroy the newborn child
out of fear for his own throne. The divine child is threatened
with persecution and pursuit, with flight and loneliness, until
later he returns in order to found a new kingdom, a kingdom of
peace and happiness for all peoples. This conflict and division
also takes place between day and night, that is, between the
rationality of our normal daily lives and the world of images and
dreams in the night.

If we open up a newspaper, watch television, or listen to the
news reports on the radio, we see the world with the eyes of the
day—familiar and well-known to us. Step by step we discover
the world of Herod, an apparently reasonable, well-ordered,
perfectly managed, and thoroughly administered world. It requires a good deal of experience and insight to see how much
this world is based upon sadism, tyranny, and violence done to

humanity. We are so used to it that we are almost immune to the pain. Only when we catch a glimpse of that to which we are truly called do we begin to resist. Then, however, the conflict is unavoidable. Not that religion itself is free from misuse by the Herods of the world!

Next to this world there is another world, the one we usually do not believe in. We have to let ourselves hear this text from Matthew in all its clarity. If Joseph had not become aware of the insanity of this day-time world by listening to and following the messages he received in the dreams of the night, then salvation would have had no chance at all in this world. We will always need to listen to the message in the background, to the dark speeches of our nights, and be ready to set out, without certainty, into the unknown. At no point can Joseph really know what will become of his life.

When the angel comes, Joseph is ordered to get up in the middle of the night and depart from a land of death. He cannot know or even guess at what awaits him in Egypt. All he knows is that he must live in a foreign land, far away from his friends and his people, a land whose language he doesn't speak and where his days are regulated by work. Isn't it possible that our lives, if we are to be saved at all, must follow the lead of our dreams, groping along from one escape from the normal and usual to the next? God has given us one promise alone: although we cannot calculate what we are or predict what will become of us, and no matter where our dreams and their instructions lead us, God will stand by us. Whether at home or in a foreign land, the angel of God will accompany us. But we must listen to him!

Since our savior came into this world these conflicts are unavoidable. Those who take their dreams seriously must risk conflict with everything in the external world of the day. And they will find that they stand confronted with the choice of what to do, either maintaining things as they are by means of planning and organizing, or accepting what cannot be planned and controlled, but only obeyed and followed. They will have to choose between being lulled to sleep by the familiar and comfortable, and setting out into the new. They will either stubbornly persist in the ghetto of fear, or cross the frontiers and break the chains.

This much is clear: a return home will only be possible once the Herods of the world are gone. But when in human history will they disappear? When will they not have their successors with different names? The medieval thinkers were wrong when they, following St. Augustine, thought that the city of God and the city of Satan, that is, the kingdom of God and the kingdoms of this world, were two coexisting entities, counterbalancing one another on God's scale. For these two realms will always contradict each other, like Cain and Abel, like day and night, like death and life, like Herod and Christ. And we are in between and must make a choice if we want to stand on the side of hope, of the light, and of fearlessness.

We have to stop exercising and straining our awesome ability to suffer. We have to put an end to the attitude that orders are orders, to the habit of doing what we are told under the rule of power, like the soldiers who fall upon the city of Bethlehem doing only what they were ordered to do, no matter what the result. Wouldn't it be much simpler and salutary to just do what God says we should do? We have no lack of feeling for dreams. We have no lack of messages in the night. It is simply a matter of putting aside our fear and doing God's will.

# Second Week
# after Christmas

## Recognizing the Needs of the Other

*"You have heard that it was said, 'An eye for an eye and a tooth for a tooth.' But I say to you, offer no resistance to one who is evil. When someone strikes you on [your] right cheek, turn the other one to him as well. If anyone wants to go to law with you over your tunic, hand him your cloak as well. Should anyone press you into service for one mile, go with him for two miles. Give to the one who asks of you, and do not turn your back on one who wants to borrow"* (Mt 5:38-42).

We will have peace in this world the moment we are able to look more upon the needs of others than on the particular ways in which they express their needs. We will be able to achieve peace when we become capable of seeing the force of disappointed love behind feelings of hatred, the sense of desecrated human dignity behind acts of violence, and the suffering of oppression behind resistance and rebellion.

The idea that the Sermon on the Mount wants to communicate to us is so simple and so logical that it is surprising how difficult it is for us to understand. If we preach it straight out as our task and duty, then we usually attain exactly the opposite of the freedom and peace we are seeking. People of good will are easily overburdened, and even the holiest doctrines can become recipes for profound guilt and depression when they are taken as moral imperatives. Not even the precept to live in peace with one another, which today is probably more important than anything else, can be put directly into practice, neither in private nor in public. How many months and years does it take to instill enough trust and self-confidence in people that they can believe they have a right to their own feelings and can dare to express what is going on within them? We humans are not capable of living in peace without a certain pride in ourselves, without a solid belief in our own dignity. We might yield to all kinds of pressure on account of pure cowardice, or we might be pushed into something, or we might be so intimidated that we don't dare speak a single bad word or do anything to cause reprobation. But what goes on inside us? Every spark of life that we do not dare to express and to live out in full takes its toll on us and on everything around us. Even the wounds caused by self-accusation and the raging of despair are products and forms of aggression, only disguised and more difficult to deal with.

Everything seems so natural and so obvious when spoken from the mouth of Jesus. He was so convinced that we could, must, and should feel like children of an eternal king, like children of our father in heaven, that to him the reasons why peace cannot be attained, reasons which seem to us so momentous, appeared completely insignificant. It is a fact that we can get involved in the most terrible competitive struggles with one another over something trivial, like the way we dress. But the motivation lying behind this is a desperate feeling of inferiority and the inability to live as we feel we should and want to live, according to our true selves. Everything appeared so simple to the eyes of Jesus, every flower lived its beauty, every bird sang its song, why couldn't we human beings do likewise? And even if someone would come and try to tear the coat off our back — and let us note that this was the only piece of outer clothing one had in ancient Israel, and that it served as protection from heat and cold by day and by night for it was coat and blanket at the same time — even if someone would come and try to take this away from us, then we are told to undress right there and hand it over. And not only that, we are to give up our other clothes as well. *Look to what the other person needs and don't try to defend yourself, for you only involve yourself in conflicts that lead to nothing.*

This is a wonderful teaching, and it is absolutely true. When people accuse us, curse us, and denounce us, then we need to listen to what it is that has hurt them, what it is that causes them to suffer. Perhaps the accusations of others seem completely absurd to us, without any justification whatever, but when we react and ourselves begin to accuse then we only make the situation worse. We transform a dialogue into a power struggle. It is no longer a question of what the other person has to say, but of who is right. And, of course, we are always right, and we will always successfully defend ourselves against unjustified charges—this much we owe to ourselves. Every person who is weak within or, in the language of the Christian Scriptures, who does not have enough faith, who is afflicted with fear and anxiety, will act in this way. Such people have to defend themselves. It requires great inner strength to feel and to see that the more others heap abuse upon us, the more they are hurting in themselves. When we understand that we do not need to feel threatened by this, we can encounter the other person openly and freely.

Jesus tells us to pray for those who persecute us. And in a certain sense this even means that we should be glad and thank God that they persecute us. For this is what Christ experienced in his own life. He knew that there is no truth we can carry into this insane world that will not immediately call forth opposition, disquiet, fear, hatred, every form of abuse, and even hell itself. But this wonderful man from Nazareth told us that we must nevertheless take the risk. One doesn't light a lamp, not even on the Christmas tree, in order to hide it. The night is dark and the world is cold, and it loves the darkness more than the light. People will try to extinguish every hope, but the light of our life is with God, and no one can take this from us.

When others force us to go a mile with them, we can always say that our path leads in another direction, and that we have nothing to do with these people anyway, and that we have more important things to do than accompany them on their wanderings. But aren't those who force us to go a mile with them people who are afraid of the road and of the unknown and of the dangers of life? Our entire life would change right here and now if we had the inner freedom to say to ourselves and to others that we are ready to go with them, wherever they want, as far

as is necessary, as long as they need us, for we are all brothers
and sisters to one another, we are all children of God. Of course
we don't know what path the others must travel, we have no
idea where they want to go, but we are asked to accompany
them. That which they think they have to get out of us with force
is really something they have a right to, for they can't do otherwise. If we could see this and live accordingly, then peace
would fall upon this earth like a gentle morning dew, and life
would spring forth from under the ashes of the fires of war.

What alternative do we have to the story at the beginning of
the Bible, the story of Cain and Abel? We belong together, we
are all brothers and sisters. But we all come into the world
wanting and needing to know why we exist and who we are. We
want to be respected by others and respected absolutely by God.
This is what Jesus wanted to teach us in place of the story of
Cain and Abel. If it is not clear to us, then we will think of the
people around us, no matter how near they may be and how
much we are bound to them, as deadly competitors. And life
will be a never-ending torment of trying to be better, more com-
petent, and more productive. We will live with the terrible hope
that the more we do, accomplish, achieve, produce, and sacrifice
on the altar of all kinds of idols, the more we will be loved,
accepted, and needed. And we will always know that there are
others who are doing better than we are. They haven't earned
it, but destiny and good luck are kinder to them. The prisons of
the world are full of people who have killed, robbed, and broken
the law in order to get something they wanted or to get rid of
something they thought was preventing them from feeling like
real human beings. The people behind bars are the ones who
make it clear to us, as our victims, how we ourselves really live.
Not a single one of them would be there if there had been people
who, instead of one mile had gone two, instead of their coats
alone had also given the shirt, who in the face of curses had
given a blessing.

These are not questions of morality. They are questions of a
new beginning. And what is our faith if not to begin again completely anew and to transform this world, which stands on the
other side of paradise, into a new creation, into a world of peace,
the beginning of the light?

## In the Beginning

*In the beginning was the Word,*
*the Word was with God*
*and the Word was God.*
*He was in the beginning with God.*
*All things came to be through him,*
*and without him nothing came to be.*
*What came to be through him was life,*
*and this life was the light of the human race;*
*the light shines in the darkness,*
*and the darkness has not overcome it (Jn 1:1-5).*

*Wisdom sings her own praises,*
*before her own people she proclaims her glory;*
*In the assembly of the Most High she opens her mouth,*
*in the presence of his hosts she declares her worth:*

*"Before all ages, in the beginning, he created me,*
*and through all ages I shall not cease to be"*
*(Sir 24:1-2, 9).*

How can John say such a thing as "In the beginning was the Word"? Only within the last two million years have the two halves of our brain evolved independently and the ability to use language developed in the left side of the brain. No one really knows how language originated. But there is a lot of evidence that suggests we learned to use words to recall experiences of very intense emotions. The farther back we look into the history of the human race, the more we encounter the word *magic*. Only words spoken in such a way that they enchant the whole world must have been used at the beginning of human history. These words have the power to awaken strong feelings and thus to make everything around us somehow different, powerful, and effectively present in our lives. Perhaps it was while dancing in ecstasy around a sacred object, an object that the dancers called to over and over, that words were born. And when the same words were later spoken, accompanied by the same call to dance, the same rhythmical motion, the same solemn and ecstatic movements, then the same emotions arose as in the presence of the holy object itself. Because words are able to awaken in us the same experiences and feelings that we had when the objects they represent were present before us, they must have gradually begun to make the objects themselves alive in us even when they were no longer actually there. Words began to build up an inner world within us independent of the external world.

This is how the history of the incarnation begins. Human consciousness acquires the ability to make itself free of the things around it. And ideas and words are more easily moved about than material objects in space. It is possible to manipulate them much more quickly than an ax or a club. It is possible to think something over, that is, to place words on top of each other so that new associations and patterns of meaning arise. Thus the human spirit is born with the ability to name all the things around us in such a way that they become subject to our control.

Beyond this, language allows us to get an idea of the world as a whole, that is, an idea of being itself, which we would never have become aware of without the ability to use language. This is the experience that the gospel of John wants to tell us about in those first sentences. We first learned to speak by verbally copying objects and by concentrating our feelings into sounds. But we discovered by doing this that all these things and the entire world must have existed long before we became aware of them. Everything we have a name for is merely a tiny aspect, a portion of the great domain of reality, a perspective that has opened up for us only within a short period of world history and its evolution. The truths we discover must always have existed. We have become aware of them only because of certain peculiarities in the development of our brains. Can we not say then, like the gospel of John, that every truth we are able to find within the world and express in language existed from the very beginning and was always there? Words are closely bound to us, but they reveal a part of reality that has existed since the beginning of time. And so they are a part of God.

As arrogant as it might sound, it is nonetheless right to say this. It also gives us a certain way of understanding the world. And when we say that the origin of human language does not simply lie in naming objects and things, but in the concentration of feelings arising in the experience of the world, then we must admit that the first way in which we understood our lives and the world must have been poetry. For only words of poetry are powerful enough and strong enough to call up feelings even when they merely speak of the things around us, of the stars, of the sun, of the trees in the wind, of the flowers and the springs of water, of the snow and the mountains. All parts of the world that exist in human language are associated with certain feelings, experiences, and images that are significant for our lives. Whenever we speak of something outside us we also mean something within, and every part of the world that is named by the word of a poet is also a piece of our soul. Therefore the gospel of John is right to bring the beginning of creation into relation with our human history. Our existence must have been intended and planned as God created this world. God must also have spoken our names and the fragility of our lives with all the gentleness and beauty with which a poem sings a part of the world.

A piece of stone lying at the bottom of a stream is shaped by the water flowing over it for perhaps thousands of years. Everything we see in it comes from its external appearance; within it is lifeless. But in the hands and the mouth of a poet this dead piece of nature becomes a work of art. It ceases to be a mere thing and receives a soul. And this is exactly what happens with our own lives. We are a piece of dust that has been breathed out and spoken by the mouth of God. And so we have become a wonderful, living work of art, endowed with a soul. There is nothing accidental or meaningless about our lives. We live because God has spoken into us, because — and let us dare to say this — our human life has taken up a part of the spirit of God and has made it live in this world and let it become visible. That which otherwise would be merely accidental, our entire life nothing but a random event in the capricious game of nature, without necessity, becomes instead something great and beautiful and receives the dignity and value of a work of art. This is what happens when God speaks to us.

The gospel of John, and the entire early church, thought that we only learned this way of seeing the world the moment we heard the words of Jesus of Nazareth and were able to listen to what he had to tell us. The way he spoke to us gave us the self-confidence and the strength to believe that our little lives expressed something of God. We were able to understand that we ourselves, with the few decades of earthly life granted us, are necessary for God to be able to speak fully into God's creation. This is the poetry, artistic feeling, and fantasy with which Jesus spoke about the life of each and every one of us. And this is why we call him the Word of God, the Word itself that God spoke to us. He taught us to listen to each other in such a way that human speech, in all its expressions of suffering and need, of joy and happiness, became able to make something of God audible in us and through us. To speak of the Word of God like this makes it possible to express our own lives in such a way that we become a word of blessing for one another, a word of thanks, and a word of prayer.

## The Name of Love

*In the beginning was the Word,*
*the Word was with God*
*and the Word was God.*
*He was in the beginning with God.*
*All things came to be through him,*
*and without him nothing came to be.*
*What came to be through him was life,*
*and this life was the light of the human race;*
*the light shines in the darkness,*
*and the darkness has not overcome it....*

*And the Word became flesh*
*and made his dwelling among us,*
*and we saw his glory,*
*the glory of the Father's only Son,*
*full of grace and truth (Jn 1:1-5, 14).*

*Wisdom sings her own praises,*
*before her own people she proclaims her glory;*
*In the assembly of the Most High she opens her mouth,*
*in the presence of his hosts she declares her worth:*

*"Before all ages, in the beginning, he created me,*
*and through all ages I shall not cease to be"*
                              *(Sir 24:1-2, 9).*

These words from John's gospel became very early in the history of the church the key that opened the doors of the philosophical schools and academies of the ancient world. If, as it is said here, Christ is the incarnate form of the rational principle of the world, the *logos* itself, then it seemed quite logical and appropriate to assume that our own reason and intellect are able to gain access to the divine mysteries. Thus it seemed the best preparation for becoming a Christian lay in education, study, and intellectual discipline. With this approach, Christianity in fact succeeded in making itself understandable to classical philosophy. But this approach also led Western culture to acknowledge the intellect alone as truly human. "The Word became flesh" came to mean that only the Word was valid and true, and that everything else that would have wanted to become flesh was barred from the gates of Christianity. It's as though we Christians have always felt ourselves obliged to divide the human brain into two halves and to claim that only the left side, with its two language centers, has a right to exist. The right side, with its images, fantasies, dreams, creativity, and holistic perception, became feared as something unchristian. Dreams and dancing, painting and music, poetry in the widest sense of the word, all these things threatened to decline and wither away in the Christian way of life.

To think this way is to misunderstand completely the gospel of John. For John takes the idea of the Word of God from Ecclesiasticus, the Book of Jesus Sirach. There was a peculiar opinion floating around at that time in Judaism that a human being could no longer bear to look directly upon God. If God were to appear to humanity, as in the first days of the human race, our weak, infirm, and fragile existence would perish at the sight of the divine countenance. After all, didn't human history begin when God had to send Adam and Eve out of paradise because of the fear and shame they felt in his presence? And didn't God have to clothe fleeing humanity in order to lessen the feelings of self-disgrace that tormented them?

Even on Sinai, as in God's self-revelation to Moses, didn't God have to shroud the divine countenance in clouds while Moses built a wall to keep the people from coming too near to the holy mountain? Even Moses had to hide his face from the radiant force of God's majestic countenance. His contemporaries could not have borne this blinding light for any length of time at all. The only thing that we are capable of perceiving of God, so it was thought in late Judaism, was a shadow of God's wisdom, the expression of God's word as it appears and is decipherable in the order of the creation and in the lofty teachings of the law. Wisdom and the Word became almost independent entities mediating between God and humanity; they were the only bridges that still remained. But how can we human beings,

as confused as our hearts are, apprehend and understand the
order of the world and the infinite wisdom of the divine law?
This is John's starting point. Is it not so that our own darkness,
the pressure and the heavy burden of despair, often keeps us
from seeing any light at all? Is it not so that the panic of our
flight is so strong that no word can reach us? John puts the
answer to these questions, to the all-consuming doubt that
haunts us, right at the beginning of his gospel. He tells that in
the beginning was the Word. Jesus Christ is the living Word of
God, and he looks at us with a human face. He has come to
teach us everything all over again — how to understand the creation, how to perceive the wisdom of the divine order, and how
to come to know of the needs of our own hearts.

How must we speak so that our words are like the word of
God addressed to us in the way Jesus spoke? There is hardly a
more important discovery in our century than that many mental
and physical illnesses appear because what goes on within us,
in our hearts, is barred from language, prevented from being
spoken out, banished from consciousness. Thus our feelings lead
an almost demonic life of their own, cut off from the rest of our
being. We can only be healthy and whole when we — each and
every one of us — have the right to express and communicate our
feelings and our longings in the images and symbols coming from
the depths of the soul. Jesus wanted to give us this freedom of
speech in the presence of God and of other people when he
freed the tongues of the dumb, opened the ears of the deaf, and
drove out the demons that robbed us of speech. He wanted us
to be self-confident enough to be able to tell each other all the
repressed thoughts and feelings in our hearts. The whole world,
everything surrounding us is to be understood as a never-ending
dialogue of mercy and kindness between God and humanity.
This is what John meant.

"In the beginning was the Word" should not at all be taken
to mean that the conceptualization of objective entities in
rational categories of thought stood at the beginning in opposition to art, painting, and music. What is being spoken of here
is a way to use language that is powerful enough to bring forth
dreams, to paint the entire world like a portrait of God and

humanity, and to bring everything to resound in harmonious song.

Everything that surrounds us has its own peculiar language. Its being has the form of a communication to us in words. The stars are not merely exploding hydrogen bombs in space, as we have been taught in physics and astronomy; they are also signs of the promise of heaven and of an eternal home. The moon, which probably arose from the cosmic dust at the same time as the other planets, is not merely a cold body orbiting around the planet earth; it is also a symbol of dreams, of love, and of the obscure contours produced by fantasy and longing. All things — the sea, the forests, the flowers, the birds — have their own words to say to us, for they are parts of our soul and have been with us for millions of years, long before we gained the ability to use language in the normal sense.

If we look more closely, then we see that every human being comes into the world with his or her own unique image, individual song, and distinctive name. This name is with God, and we must learn it in the course of the few decades we are given to live upon this earth. How must we speak to one another so that feelings are expressed, fears quieted, illnesses healed, so that our words are devout enough to be a prayer and human enough to build bridges of understanding? How much remains unsaid merely because we have no name for love? How many conflicts remain unresolved merely because we have never learned to talk about our problems without having to fear injury and destruction?

The most beautiful and the most human thing we can do is to discover a way of speaking that becomes painting, music, and dream, and which expresses the entire breadth and depth of our hearts and thus the entire creation. In the beginning was the Word and the Word dwelt among us.

# Epiphany

## Follow the Star

*When Jesus was born in Bethlehem of Judea, in the days of King Herod, behold, magi from the east arrived in Jerusalem, saying, "Where is the newborn king of the Jews? We saw his star at its rising and have come to do him homage." When King Herod heard this, he was greatly troubled, and all Jerusalem with him. Assembling all the chief priests and the scribes of the people, he inquired of them where the Messiah was to be born. . . . Then Herod called the magi secretly and ascertained from them the time of the star's appearance. He sent them to Bethlehem and said, "Go and search diligently for the child. When you have found him, bring me word, that I too may go and do him homage." After their audience with the king they set out. And behold, the star that they had seen at its rising preceded them, until it came and stopped over the place where the child was. They were overjoyed at seeing the star, and on entering the house they saw the child with Mary his mother. They prostrated themselves and did him homage. Then they opened their treasures and offered him gifts of gold, frankincense, and myrrh. And having been warned in a dream not to return to Herod, they departed for their country by another way (Mt 2:1-4, 7-12).*

In a certain sense the Eastern Church is right to celebrate this day of the manifestation of the Lord as the real feast of Christmas. For the truth of our salvation is not merely that the savior was born, but whether or not we take him into our hearts. God is everywhere, but as close to us or as far away as we choose. The feast of Epiphany, the manifestation of the Lord, asks us

how God is present and visible in our lives, and how we can see
his light in the middle of our normal, everyday world.

A sacred text concerning the way God becomes visible in the
world can speak to us on only two levels. There is the level of
the world, one we know all too well, even to the point of despair.
It is represented by King Herod, and its place is Jerusalem.
Everything we read in the daily newspapers fits into the chronicles and accounts of this sort of history. It is a world in which
people rule over one another, dominate each other, a world in
which people can only be certain of life when they have acquired
enough power and control over others to torment and plague
them.

In this world we can escape fear of others and feel secure
only when we have the power necessary to hold others in check.
For those who rule in this world, other people are like dumb
animals to train and control with the whip of fear and to discipline by commands that they have to obey. They either fight
back or are forced to run for their lives. This is a world of
opportunism and betrayal of humanity, but it is so normal, so
terribly normal, that we have difficulty imagining any other
world. Everything is fair game, and almost everything belongs
to the strongest: women belong to men, children belong to
women, the employees belong to bosses, and the people belong
to their rulers. Everything is property and belongs to someone,
and humanness itself is sold to the highest bidder. In this sort
of world people are ordinary, lowly, and exploitable. By manipulation of their instincts, they can be led about on a leash and
held under control.

This way of thinking, feeling, and acting is cheap and vulgar;
it is the world of Herod. But don't think that God isn't spoken
of in this world. The powerful talk a lot about religion in this
world, but only as a means of domination, as an instrument by
which to exercise still more power. King Herod and those like
him don't hesitate for a moment to consult the holy books in
order to inform themselves, but their purpose is to spy out their
enemy with the eagle eye of hate and find out how best to attack
and destroy that enemy, that threat to their power. Of course
this world is—must be—threatened by everything that comes
from God. For what comes from God is the freedom and great-

ness of humanity. This always places the self-appointed idols into question. They have to defend themselves in order to survive, and they can be terrible when fighting for their lives. Even gestures of devotion can serve as a disguise for the interests of power. Even religion itself can be nothing more than an ideology enslaving people and making them dependent, an instrument of deception, alienation, terror, and intimidation.

We don't need to say much about this world, for we all know it well. We live in it every day. We breathe its atmosphere to the point of suffocation. It conditions us, determines our daily lives, and it would seem inescapable to us if we didn't know that there was another world beyond it.

By God's grace, however, we are capable of travelling the path of the magi and returning to ourselves. It is a path that begins with the longings of dark and lonely nights. It arises from the question of how we can discover the divine in the realm of the human, how we can learn to see people as messengers of God and take them into our hearts. It is a question of how we can become capable of looking at people in such a way that they shine forth with the glory of God. This is what really counts. It can be learned from the magi of the East, people who can feel the unseen, read what is hidden to the eye, and understand dreams.

On this level everything depends upon our believing more in the language of our longings than in the world of external facts. Our forgotten dreams speak more truly of human reality than anything we can learn from the actions of the mighty in this world. Our heart is more deeply formed by its secret and hidden desires than by the pressure of those who stand outside. All the magic of religion, all the enchantment of the heart begins with the discovery of ourselves—the yearnings that sustain us, the expectations that influence us, and the concealed hopes that guide us.

There are times in the darkness of night, in the midst of loneliness, disorientation, and despair, when it is possible to discover our star. It rises as if on the other side of the world. Perhaps it seems inconspicuous at first. Nevertheless we dare to follow, yes, we believe we *must* follow no matter what deserts and wildernesses full of dangers must be crossed. We have to be ready to travel this road, following the star that appears in the western sky. The dawn is still far away, but we can see a light in the distance, a tiny shimmer of hope. We follow this light, and we discover that there are ancient prophecies, old writings that speak of a savior who is to come.

Written in the heart of every single person is a truth that wants to live. Its message is transcribed upon the heart as if upon old, faded pages. This unique truth belongs to us as individuals; it tells us about the reality of our happiness and what we must wait for in order to fulfill our destiny. There comes a moment for each person where the inner world and the outer world confront each other, a moment of terrible fear and anguish. What will those who are out in the world say—the kings, the mighty, the powers surrounding us, the frightening forces of our environment—when we set out with the fantastic faith in dreams and stars, when we say that we have come a long way to find a child, an unformed, hidden existence upon which the shimmer of the divine rests? Won't we merely look ridiculous? Won't we be putting ourselves into danger? Won't we be playing into the hands of our enemies? The magi dared to do this, to come to their fellow king in Jerusalem and to see the star before them and follow it till it came to rest. They found the place that they were seeking, the place of their longing and their promise.

Then comes the task of learning to bow down before that which seems so small in the heart of others, before the unbroken goodness and beauty that lives in them, of bowing with humility and with devotion before the life beginning in them and the growing happiness within their hearts. For the language of love sees the star of God shining above the head of each person and discovers the glory of God in his or her heart. As if in a gesture of adoration, it reverently kneels down before the happiness and joy that appear in the other person's heart. Then our own heart comes to rest and our own longing knows that it has found its fulfillment.

There is a lot of speculation about the gifts the magi brought to the child in Bethlehem. I believe we can understand these three gifts in terms of the old Egyptian inscriptions that record the pharaohs' wishes for their queens: May you live long; may you prosper; may you be happy.

May you live long. This is symbolized by myrrh, which was used for healing illnesses and alleviating pain. Myrrh symbolizes the wish that the life of others here on earth will be free, as much as possible, from pain, illness, and suffering. We wish our own existence, to the extent of our abilities, to be for those we touch like myrrh, that is, that we lessen their pain, take away their suffering, and heal their sicknesses.

Frankincense symbolizes the wish that this heavenly scent rise in the heart of others, that their hearts may be allowed to flower and bloom, that they may open to the heavens and to the light. With the offering of incense we wish that life grows and develops and becomes like perfume, that everything beautiful becomes visible and manifests itself for the joy of all who can see and appreciate it.

And finally there is gold. Whenever we gain a feeling for our own worth, our own inestimable value, greatness, and beauty, then our heart grows and expands in joy. This is what we wish to give others, to somehow communicate to them, and we wish that our own lives contribute to this.

It is told that the magi received a message in a dream to return home. If this happens in our lives, it would be a dream come true. For by staying together, we are at home in the hearts of one another.

## The Gifts of the Magi

*Then they opened their treasures and offered him gifts of gold,
frankincense, and myrrh. And having been warned in a dream
not to return to Herod, they departed for their country by
another way (Mt 2:11-12).*

The story of the magi is not a historical report. It didn't
happen like an event we read about in the newspapers. Herod
is a historical figure though. People like him rule with the scepter
of power. If someone were to tell such a Herod that a king of
the heart will be born, a king whose power is based upon the
gentleness of his words, the magic of his love, and his ability to
enchant the hearts of men and women, Herod would call
together all the intellectuals and those representing established
religion for advice on how to get rid of this savior before he
could cause trouble. We find this kind of farce in the newspapers
when we see how the mighty make a show of honoring religion
only to exploit it and suppress it. They join their hands as if in
prayer while actually using them to kill. They inform themselves
under the pretense that they also wish to subject themselves to
the true ruler of the world, but really they are only interested
in trampling him under their feet. This is history.

Thank God that the history we read in the newspapers and
the history books is not the only history there is. There is another
level upon which we can speak about humanity, and it is at least
as true, and probably much more true, than what we usually
mean by history, for it appears in the depths of the soul. We
call the stories of this kind of human history legends or fairy
tales. Perhaps only the fairy tales themselves believe that fairy
tales can be true, and maybe only legends think it is possible for
people to be pure and true and loyal to themselves and to their
creator. But this has to be true, if God is to appear at all, for
the beauty of God remains unseen unless it is reflected in the
beauty of human faces and in the truth of their hearts.

But how do we discover the beauty of another person and
the truth of his or her heart? This is what the story of the magi

tells us. Christianity was right to dress up the story and transform it into a fairy tale. Magicians and astrologers are not enough to conjure up the truth of a person, for human beings are kings when they follow their star; and so the astrologers became kings. And there had to be three of them searching for the fourth. And one of the three had to be dark skinned, for in all such legends the third prince is related to the night, to dreams, and to the earth. These stories describe a search for humanity, a pilgrimage to the heart, a journey to discover God in human form. Shouldn't we believe that there is a star standing above the cradle of every person, that a star shows each of us where we have really come from, a star that leads us to the path by which we can return home? The longing for paradise is rooted so deeply within us that we couldn't live a single second without the vision of our eternal home, a vision that shines for us when the nights are dark, because it is often closer to us in dreams, yearnings, and obscure feelings than in the light of day and consciousness.

We all relive this story within ourselves. We carry within us a King Herod, who defends himself with the vanity of his reason, with calculating cleverness, and with the deliberations of so-called realism. Before we can reach our true form, we will unavoidably feel threatened by this king-like ego with its violence, its power, and its external constraints. Every time we are close to the enchanted land of fantasy, the song of poetry, and the reverberation of the heart, this king will rise up on his throne snorting with rage, stamping his feet, and shouting loudly through the halls that neither feelings, nor dreams, nor longings of the heart, nor any ideas of this kind are fitting and proper and acceptable in this world.

King Herod demands conformity! We could almost pray that an angel of the Lord would appear to each person with a warning to flee from this king. Indeed, we will only be able to return home by making a big detour around this fearful prince. We must leave proud Jerusalem with its high walls in order to find small Bethlehem and truly follow the star of our destiny.

There are wonderful promises in our hearts, written by the finger of God, for the Eternal One wanted us to live and to be. God wanted not only being, but also appearance and manifestation. We could imagine that the earth stood still and the stars stopped in their course when the magi and the kings bowed down before the child and worshipped him. Only when we today become capable of seeing greatness and discovering our calling in what is not yet perfect, in what is unfinished, and in what is only beginning, will our world find peace. When we no longer despise what is small and insignificant, but instead see its true greatness; when we become aware that there is no above and below, but only this one world that God created, and that what is below is not for that reason lowly and what is high up has no right to be proud; and when we come to understand that everything fits together under the hand of God that encompasses the whole, then—and only then—this world will find harmony and completeness.

The legend tells us that the magi brought gifts of gold, frankincense, and myrrh. When a gift is fitting and tastefully chosen, it expresses the essence of the other person. We can actually only give each other what already is present in the other person and what this person embodies. What would life be like if we were allowed to believe that each one of us should be given such gifts from the very moment of birth? What would it mean if we could believe that our whole life consists in nothing but letting the pictures of these gifts grow and become manifest?

The magi laid gold at the feet of the child Jesus, gold born in the white-hot smelting furnaces of the stars. When the stars are squeezed together under enormous pressure and unimaginable temperature, they explode and throw their heavy elements into space. Later, planets are formed around new suns and traces of gold lie within their rocks. This metal will not enter into combination with other elements; it will remain pure forever. Perhaps what is most precious in our hearts has been born in this very same way, under the pressure of enormous suffering, a product of cataclysmic forces discharging within us. There are traces of this gold to be discovered in each of us. We find more of it the more we love a person.

It is necessary for us to learn to see each other with the eyes of God in order to discover God in one another. If we do this, we see that every person is as precious as gold. There is something in all of our lives that makes us into royalty, into people who are worthy, rich, and great, for our life comes from the stars.

The child Jesus was also given frankincense. The ancient Egyptians called it "that which makes divine," and when they spoke of frankincense they painted a picture of a human soul flying like a golden bird on its way back to the stars. This is also what we human beings are. We are carried by the power of longing, driven by a yearning for our true home in eternity. We are called to return to the place whence we came. And both of these, the heaviness of gold and the lightness of frankincense, live within us and we are entirely both of them.

In between is myrrh, the earthly path of our temporality and our mortality. We travel this path together. Here we can do much to comfort the human heart, to heal the pain, to lessen the suffering, and to awaken hope and strength so that we may all reach eternity.

An old Russian legend tells of a fourth king. He heard in his kingdom in Russia that the Ruler of Eternity had been born into the world, and he set out to find him. He took as gifts the most beautiful linen, bleached in the cold snow upon the mountains of his country; the most wonderful pearls from the bottoms of the shimmering streams; and honey from the most precious flowers and blossoms in the fields of the steppes.

The legend tells us that this king had not travelled far before he met poverty and sickness on the road. He offered his cloth so that the lepers could cool the heat of their fever and the fire of the sickness upon their wounded flesh with the linen bleached by the coolness of the snow from the mountains of his land. He gave his honey to a woman who had nothing to feed her child, and he distributed his pearls in a village struck by famine.

Finally, he had nothing left to offer the unknown king he was seeking. Even the star he was following in the heavens sank before his eyes, and he became a lonely wanderer, like so many men and women who have lost hope. Since he had nothing left to give, he gave thirty years of his own life for the son of a woman who had been condemned to slavery in the galleys. Broken, tattered, and beaten he finally came to Jerusalem, thirty-three years too late to pay homage to the newborn king, but soon enough to recognize the King of Eternity on the cross.

A human being deserves everything we can give, and the God who appears in the beauty of a human life wants our kindness, our compassion, and our understanding without limits, just as God is without limits. All the wealth of our hands will be still more precious when it is a gift offered to the greatness in those we love. God is there for us to recognize in the faces of poverty and smallness.

# The End and the Beginning

*"Go, therefore, and make disciples of all nations, baptizing them in the name of the Father, and of the Son, and of the holy Spirit, teaching them to observe all that I have commanded you. And behold, I am with you always, until the end of the age" (Mt 28:19-20).*

The gospel of Matthew closes with these words of the risen Christ. It is our task to tell all peoples about the chance for humanity, the chance to live a truly human life, a chance that came into this world with Christ. This means the end of thinking within the narrow borders imposed by nation and tradition, by culture and institution; it is the beginning of an opening without limits. What Matthew formulates as the final goal of his entire gospel, he also puts into the story of the childhood of Jesus as its foundation and support. He does this to make it clear that it is the nature of Jesus to speak of God in such a way that people of all places and times can hear the message personally. No one had ever spoken this way before. Even in the days of Jesus, people argued about whether it was possible to believe in God. Will the messiah come only if Israel is faithful to the law? Will it be necessary first to overcome the tyranny of the oppressors and the injustice of violence, even with violent means if all else fails?

Jesus' shocking and amazingly gentle message was that we could look up to God in such a way that our hearts became open enough to love all people. "But that doesn't work!" people answered. "We can love the people of Israel, we can love the chosen people, the children of Abraham, and we can stand up for the God of Israel alone. But we can't at the same time love those who hate us, the Romans. That would be betrayal of God!"

Talk like this reveals a division between the love of God and the love of our fellow men and women. Shortly after Jesus, this kind of thinking again gained ground, against his will and also against his words. Even today in the church we are not completely free of the tendency to build hard fronts, draw boundaries, close ourselves in, and split up into parties violently opposing one another. We have tried to bring the good news of Jesus to the peoples of the earth, but supported by the arms of conquering battalions. We annihilated cultures in order to give glory to God and proclaim the gospel of Jesus. It seems that the proclamation needed force and money and was only able to make itself understood by means of intimidation and fear.

Even today this process goes on in a spiritual way. When we speak of Christ, the first thing we try to do is show that all other religions and cultures are wrong and must be taught the truth by us. *They* don't know anything. *They* have to listen. *They* have to learn the language of our culture. *We* are the ones who are right, the chosen people; we possess the truth for all times!

It is deeply disquieting to read the gospel of Matthew and to find that he projected these ideas back into the beginning, into the childhood of Jesus. He shows us the way we have to approach Jesus. In Israel those from far away were considered ignorant pagans. Yet they are the ones who come freely to seek Jesus. They have the knowledge and wisdom through their astrology to discover the light of the star and follow it through dreamy nights. They understand these pictures of the soul to be more true and real than anything they might learn from external reality.

*This* is how faith in the incarnation of Jesus of Nazareth begins. There is something in all men and women that seeks him and wants to understand him from within, if only it is allowed to speak and is not hindered! It is possible that those who are the most ignorant in external matters are the wisest in matters of the heart. Don't we feel this in ourselves? Don't we experience the longing to break out and the desire to follow our dreams *just once* instead of binding ourselves to the truth and reality of the outside world? This feeling is communicated in the language that all peoples of all times have understood—the language of fairy tales, legends, and myths.

The Christian legend tells the story of three kings—no longer three astrologers. The number three comes from the three offerings, gold, frankincense, and myrrh. But this story exists in all cultures. Many peoples tell the story of three princes who set out upon a journey to distant lands in order to seek salvation. And in seeking, all the powers and abilities of the soul are concentrated. We become aware of the royal dignity and the golden glory that rests upon every human life, and this knowledge is one of the greatest gifts we can give each other. We become capable of perceiving the shining greatness of others in the middle of poverty and reflecting it so that they may also come to know who they are. We are able, as the image of frankincense tells us, to raise up a human life in the same way that the perfumed smoke of an evening sacrifice rises up from the earth to the heavens. And when we do this then our own life becomes like a prayer of freedom that climbs unhindered to the clouds.

It is also possible for us to speak a language of compassion and comfort to one another. This is represented in the image of myrrh. It symbolizes a language that alleviates pain to the point of numbness. And all of this—the beauty and the unity with the divine as well as the lowliness of our suffering—encompasses what it means to be human.

The Christian legend even incorporates that part of the universal myth that speaks of the third prince as somehow different from the other two, as somehow of lesser dignity, of another color and race. In the myth it is he, the dark Moor, who is closest to the savior, and this turns the world we know upside-down. This is the entire significance of the appearance of the Lord, and it seizes the mighty ones upon their thrones with fear and anxiety. It negates the logic of all that we call history, and all that we read about every day in the newspapers, and all that too often goes on in our own cruel hearts.

In response to the appearance of the savior King Herod, who is outside us and also within us, proves dangerously active again and again. The problem is not that Herod doesn't know about God, that there are not priests and theologians in great numbers at his court. The problem is that he uses God for purposes of power and in the end exploits religion in order to gain domination over others and make himself secure. King Herod does a lot for religion. He decorates the temple with gold, establishes the entire contemporary study of theology, and poses as a generous and eager patron of the church. And religion eats out of his hand, when it can, in thankfulness and dependency like a well-trained dog. But the good news of God does not tolerate people ruling over one another. It exposes us to liberation — and to the anxiety and uncertainty that overcome us the moment we are no longer treated like animals but must take upon ourselves the risk of being free.

We all have a King Herod inside of us. He worships only to kill, and he is deceitful enough to inquire about the way to the child of Bethlehem for the purpose of destroying whatever of salvation he finds there and annihilating the humanity that is newly springing forth. We have to decide, each of us individually and the entire church as a whole, whether we are on the side of the magi or of Herod in Jerusalem. Yes, in the end it is a question of once again following the dreams that warn us to change our path, escape from the pursuers, and find our way back home.

When we read the story of Jesus of Nazareth with the eye of the heart, as divine poetry, and with the fantasy of human longing, then we see that this indeed is how it began. The promise will be fulfilled when dreams become more important than the decrees and commands of those who have the say in this world, or who would have the say, if we let them.

# Learning To See with Jesus' Eyes

*"Blessed are the poor in spirit,*
  *for theirs is the kingdom of heaven.*
*Blessed are they who mourn,*
  *for they will be comforted.*
*Blessed are the meek,*
  *for they will inherit the land.*
*Blessed are they who hunger and thirst for righteousness,*
  *for they will be satisfied.*
*Blessed are the merciful,*
  *for they will be shown mercy.*
*Blessed are the clean of heart,*
  *for they will see God.*
*Blessed are the peacemakers,*
  *for they will be called children of God.*
*Blessed are they who are persecuted for the sake of*
  *righteousness,*
  *for theirs is the kingdom of heaven"* (Mt 5:3-10).

The stories that the evangelists tell about the birth of Jesus
are not intended to be historical reports. Rather, the evangelists
want to describe Jesus of Nazareth in essence—who he is for
all times. This is why they place the experiences they had with
Jesus back into the events of his birth. Everything begins with
scenes that will repeat themselves later inside the men and
women who enter into and are bound up within the sphere of
influence of the man from Nazareth.

The story of the conflict between the magicians from the
Orient and the Jewish king with his scribes may appear out of
date to us. But the early Christians had the bitter experience of
trying to communicate faith in Jesus as the messiah to the chosen
people, Israel. In this legend of the beginning of the life of Jesus
this conflict already seems to reflect an unbridgeable, deadly
antagonism. The king of the Jews kills the king of the Jews—
and the administrators of Jewish religion stand by his side and
help him by interpreting the law in such a way that it becomes

a weapon in the struggle against the One who has come to fulfill all of the prophecies made to Israel. This is said in a bitter and painful way, and also perhaps in an unjust and one-sided way.

On the other hand, the great hope remains that those who are not especially chosen, the pagans, the peoples of the earth, will come in great numbers from far away to the place of the true king. They will come not to Jerusalem, but to Bethlehem. And thus the oldest promise of the prophets will be fulfilled. What was at first intended for Israel will come to fulfillment in the church. This is what Matthew tells us in this story. But what does his story about the conflict between the magi and the Jews mean for those of us who do not come from the chosen people, but from the pagans? It poses this question: Will we decide to worship the Lord, or will we try to kill that which can give us true life? The entire confrontation between Herod and the astrologers lies in our own soul. And so we begin to read the story again and to understand it beyond its time as an image of our own time and of what goes on within our own hearts.

When we hear today that we should preach the gospel to the new pagans in the Western world, we wonder almost despairingly where we can begin. The life of modern Western men and women appears to be almost entirely determined by the struggle for external happiness, by materialism, consumerism, and by what may be called an absolutely irreligious anti-Christianity. In our world there are no kings who dare to wander about following a star, setting out upon a holy pilgrimage straight across all the deserts and lonely regions to the place where the star comes to rest. Our world is pragmatic, calculable, and controllable. There is nothing holy within it, and the only miracles that exist are the ones we are able to produce ourselves. We have become hard, and the truth is that we suffocate and smother a good deal of life.

Perhaps we know about religion in the same way that Herod knew about it. We have heard the Holy Scriptures ever since kindergarten and have learned to repeat parts of them by heart. But what they tell us is distorted to serve some form of egoism and self-assertion. In the end we know everything but understand nothing; we have learned much but have never gained wisdom; and we stand upon the pulpits, tribunes, and rostrums of this world with no idea what to say.

But human beings are more than this. The wonderful stories about the first days of Jesus tell us that he sees us in a completely different way. We are capable of understanding holy myths. Clearly, much of what we hear in such stories appears to our rational consciousness as nothing more than superstition and nonsense. Who is really interested in following stars? In fact, it is not at all a matter of astrology or whether a comet appeared at a certain time in Mesopotamia. These questions don't interest us today. What concerns us are the figures that come to us in the night, visions that can tell us who we are destined to be and where we going, if only we can understand them.

There are moments of loneliness at dusk when it becomes clear to us that we must set out and not rest until we have found what we are searching for. The question for us is how to discover ourselves again as men and women. On the surface we are closed, satisfied, and one-dimensional, but in our true depths we are, and must be, restless, confused people whose real desires are never fulfilled. Every one of us is aware of this in our own way. Much of what we seem so certain of is merely a disguise for our own uncertainty, and much of our show of being big and strong is merely compensation for the smallness and weakness in us.

We might suppose that the key to understanding the story of the magi lies in the three gifts they present to the child Jesus. Since the days of the Fathers of the church, the usual explanation has been that gold, frankincense, and myrrh represent three different ways of acknowledging Jesus as Lord. Gold represents the majesty and royal dignity of Christ; frankincense is a confession of his divinity; and myrrh is the acknowledgment of his humanity. This is a pious and orthodox interpretation, but hardly accurate. Matthew would not have entrusted his magi with the theological formulations of the fifth century. Beyond that, it does not correspond to the way in which we give offerings that are intended to express something of who we are and what feelings we bear within our hearts. People offered animal sacrifices to the gods in order to express that they themselves were like animals; they drove scapegoats into the desert in order to say that they themselves were sinful animals and should be sent away. Sacrifices *always* say something about those who offer them. Thus we see a marvelous image of ourselves in the gifts of the magi; we human beings go out seeking God and we find him, as Jesus Christ taught us, in these three symbols, in gold, frankincense, and myrrh.

There is a way of looking at people so that we see them with the dreaming eyes of night; they appear as if painted upon a golden background with the shimmer of heaven surrounding them. Seen with the eyes of day such a person might be insignificant, a nobody, a person whose life is a mess. There may be many good reasons to think that he or she will never change, never amount to anything. But if we look more closely with the eyes of love and with the eyes of a dream, as love teaches us to do, then we see that the person is called to a royal destiny.

We see a king's crown rise above the often maltreated head and the tangle of confused ideas; we see that majesty and freedom want to take root in the person and determine his or her true life. This is the way that Jesus wanted us to see others and ourselves as well. In the gospel of Matthew he demands of us — and he believes that we are capable of doing this — that we refuse to allow others to humiliate and dominate us by means of terror and fear. Do not fear others and do not hide the truth you bear within you. God watches over you and protects you. You are more valuable than anything on earth. You are held in the hand of the eternal king. These are the words and the images that Jesus of Nazareth gave us.

We all have something in us that was born in the smelting furnace of the stars, that was sown with the dust of the cosmos and condensed again so that we could come to be. It is something that withstands time. It does not combine with other things, and it lasts as a pure metal through the millennia. Something like this is in every one of us. We are like something that has fallen to earth from heaven and which has been found again in its depths.

It is only a question of what we want to see, the dust of this passing world or the gold of our true dignity. What God lets us find in ourselves is our own greatness; it is that which is most precious in us that wants to go and pay homage to God. We do not teach people to be pious and devout by pointing out how miserable and insignificant they are. Instead, we must let them find their way back to that which is most valuable in themselves. For what each of us has to offer is nothing less than gold, and it is the force within us that drives us on until we find God in this world. This is how Jesus of Nazareth lived, and he wanted us to live this way too.

The same is true for frankincense. Probably none of the ancient peoples knew the meaning of frankincense better than the culture of the pharaohs on the Nile. When they spoke of frankincense, they used a word that means "that which makes divine." When the kernels of incense were burned at the evening sacrifice and their perfume rose toward heaven, then something "became" divine. And so the ancient Egyptians drew the human soul like a vessel filled with incense, whose sacred cloud rose up toward heaven. The human soul itself was "that which makes divine," and it was an offering pleasing to God. This is what the ancient Egyptians thought. They saw the eternal desire to transcend the small circle of this world, an infinite longing that arises and climbs and yearns to return to the stars.

We can look at one another merely to find out where we came from and who we are now. The more we are pressed into these definitions of the moment, the determinations of the present day, the more we become like animals in a trap, without a way out or a way back, walled in by the conventions and formalities that regulate our lives. This can go so far that we almost completely lose the feeling we have for our true origin and for our own history. We are what we are, the brute facts and nothing more, and we can't do anything about it. We never were anything else, and we will never become anything more. Much of what we think about people runs directly into the jaws of this trap, which has an enormous power to constrict people, even to the point of death. We no longer know anything about a journey from the East.

But there are other visions of humanity, those that come in the night. Then we feel and know that this small earth will never satisfy us, and that we are the most insatiable, most demanding, most hopeful, and for that very reason often the most desperate beings upon this planet. What does not come from eternity fails to fulfill our desires. What does not come from God does not count as true for us. To see people in this way, in the longing of their hearts, in their desire for a truth that is never fully present but only gradually coming is a wonderful vision of humanity. It means seeing people in the courage of their questioning, their doubting, their deep searching, and in their need constantly to go further. To offer incense in this way does not mean to set oneself up in a ceremonious world in which everything is already explained, all questions already answered, all the information already given, a world of rote memory and thoughtless repetition. It means to have the courage to ask questions to which no answers have yet been found. When we do this, something in us is burned in such a way that, although it is destroyed, it gives off a scent of heaven in this world. This is how we are. Always breaking out, always full of longing for truth and for love more than anything else. As Jesus said, Blessed are those who hunger and thirst for God and justice. They are blessed before God because they are hungry—ravenous for the eternal good. This is how Jesus saw a person bringing frankincense to Bethlehem.

After the gold and the incense, the symbol of myrrh makes sense. We human beings are weak, always standing near the edge of the precipice, always close to destruction. We can be moved to give up every dream of God and the poetry of love by a simple bodily pain. We need to experience only a single disappointment in order to let the heavens collapse around us. If the temperature of our bodies rises by only a few degrees, we are subject to feverish delusions. We are exposed, sensitive, easily breakable beings who constantly run to doctors for healing, to places that alleviate our pain, to drugs and narcotics, that is, to myrrh. We need it always. If we understand this image properly, and don't use it to humiliate ourselves, then it can teach us to be compassionate toward each other and not to demand *more* than we can give.

In the eyes of Jesus we can count on being accepted for what we are, mere human beings, or, in the language of his time, beings formed of clay and water, beings who are so fragile, often so weak that the first thing we need in our confusion is a word of understanding, compassion, and guidance.

Jesus formulates his message quite clearly. Twice he says in the gospel of Matthew that he doesn't want any sacrifices; instead, we should go and learn what it means to be merciful. And Matthew paints the great picture of how it will be at the end of time when the peoples of the world, like the three magi, come to their secret king from all the ends of the earth. Then the only questions that count will be these: What works of compassion are we capable of doing? How can we lessen the misery of others with the myrrh of our tenderness and sympathy? It is not true that we human beings are far away from God. God dwells in the greatness of humanity, in the power of our longing, and in the gentleness of our pity. It was in order to give us these things that Jesus of Nazareth came into this world.

# After Epiphany

## Visions and Dreams

*When the days were completed for their purification according
to the law of Moses, they took him up to Jerusalem to present
him to the Lord, just as it is written in the law of the Lord,
"Every male that opens the womb shall be consecrated to the
Lord," and to offer the sacrifice of "a pair of turtledoves or
two young pigeons," in accordance with the dictate in the law
of the Lord.*

*Now there was a man in Jerusalem whose name was Sim-
eon. This man was righteous and devout, awaiting the con-
solation of Israel, and the holy Spirit was upon him. It had
been revealed to him by the holy Spirit that he should not see
death before he had seen the Messiah of the Lord. He came
in the Spirit into the temple; and when the parents brought in
the child Jesus to perform the custom of the law in regard to
him, he took him into his arms and blessed God, saying:*

> *"Now, Master, you may let your servant go in peace,*
> *according to your word,*
> *for my eyes have seen your salvation,*
> *which you prepared in sight of all the peoples,*
> *a light for revelation to the Gentiles,*
> *and glory for your people Israel" (Lk 2:22-32).*

What do we expect from our lives?
A short time ago a young man said to me:

Do you know, I haven't been able to sleep well for years.
I wake up in the middle of the night bathed in sweat. I

214

must have been dreaming something right before, but I can never remember anything in detail. Also, during the day I avoid ever really relaxing. Somehow I constantly have the feeling that my life is slipping away from me, as if something crucial has to happen, but I can't reach it. It's as though I were running after a train that is moving faster and faster away from me. I can't go on living like this.

On the other hand a woman told me that all she wants to do is sleep. She said:

What I would really like to do is just go to sleep. I often feel so tired that I just close my eyes and hope to wake up in another world. What do I have to hope for in this world? Everything is so dark and gray and hopeless. If there is anything better, then it has to be in heaven.

It often seems to me that our lives vacillate between two poles, which are seldom so clearly formulated as in these two statements. We swing back and forth, more or less confused, between the restlessness of unfulfilled expectations on the one side and the hopelessness of a not yet final resignation on the other. We seem to pose as cynical and disillusioned or to show ourselves to others as if we were full of will power and strength. In the one case, we overburden ourselves; in the other, we force ourselves to become resigned.

Simeon, the old man in this passage from the gospel of Luke, stands directly in the middle between the two poles. He clearly experiences something wonderful in this moment of grace in the Temple, when the promise to all Israel, the messiah, is laid right into his arms and into his heart. But it seems to me that his entire life is something even more wonderful than this moment of fulfillment. What sort of man is this who believes, or knows from God, that he will not die until his eyes have seen the savior? Certainly Simeon knew no more than any other man or woman how his life would turn out. He undoubtedly had as many reasons for resignation as anyone else. He surely had his own setbacks; his needs and disappointments were no less than those of other people. But still Simeon held to a hope for his earthly life, which was slipping away from him so quickly, in fact, already approaching its end. His was not a hope for another world, but a hope for *this* life, for this sad, afflicted, and plagued world.

How can we become capable of holding on to our hopes against all appearances, against everything that we see about us? How do we learn to wait for the light in the middle of darkness? Luke is completely right that this ability cannot come from us alone. To others, Simeon was a dreamer. They probably said that he was deluded; that he was old enough to know better, to be realistic about life, to let go of his childish dreams of a coming salvation; and that it is more important to see reality as it is. But Simeon obviously had never ceased being like a child — full of dreams, hopes, and expectations. Above all, he must have known that we can never be satisfied with anything less than God. For a wonderful dream, the vision of a divine child lies within each of us, imprinted into our nature.

This symbol of hope lived within Simeon's heart. He felt that his life was so original, so pure, and so truly sustained and accepted by God that heaven had touched the earth. We must also believe in something like this, or everything around us will sink into darkness. A vision like this has to live within us, or we will not possess the strength to live upon this earth. What God intended for us must grow and become strong within us. There may indeed be much that is false and corrupt in us, but there is still this vision of the child that God wants us to be.

What makes Simeon so happy in this moment in the Temple? What does he hold in his arms? There is nothing here to satisfy any kind of demand for proof. A child, that is all. But it is precisely this that gives hope. He holds a child, not something already finished and complete, but a human form, which can develop and grow. This is what Israel had been promised, and this is what has been given to each and every one of us to take with us along our way.

In the days of the prophets of Israel, Joel foretold that at the end of time the old people would be given the power to see visions and the young would receive the ability to dream. Never again would people need to be taught about God from others, for God would communicate directly to the heart capable of perceiving truth.

What happens to an old person who is granted the vision of God? Looking back, such a person sees that his or her whole life falls into place, that it receives a center and forms itself into a picture made up of many parts, that it appears like a road coming to its end, that it is a path along which God has accompanied the person, silently and often unseen, but always present. Such people feel a growing thankfulness, and they can look back upon their earthly life as if from the vantage point of heaven. But even more, they can see beyond the dark wall of death, for the image of the child in the arms of an old man is a promise of immortality, of eternal life, and of heaven.

Everything that is true begins here on this earth. Everything that the promise of God has set as a goal before us is already present in our hearts. God will never send us away without the pictures of fulfilled hope. We can live in peace here in this afflicted and threatened world.

The face of God struggles within us to come into the light; God's nature grows into a revelation that can only communicate itself to the world in and through us. Every one of us has the right to see this revelation, but we need holy places, temples for the things of this earth, rooms in which we are so near the divine that we can feel all God's promises rise up within our souls like a song, like a prayer, like never-ending praise poured forth over the world and over our own lives.

## The Heavens Are Open

> *Now the people were filled with expectation, and all were ask-*
> *ing in their hearts whether John might be the Messiah. John*
> *answered them all, saying, "I am baptizing you with water,*
> *but one mightier than I is coming. I am not worthy to loosen*
> *the thongs of his sandals. He will baptize you with the holy*
> *Spirit and fire." . . . After all the people had been baptized*
> *and Jesus also had been baptized and was praying, heaven*
> *was opened and the holy Spirit descended upon him in bodily*
> *form like a dove. And a voice came from heaven, "You are*
> *my beloved Son; with you I am well pleased" (Lk 3:15-16,*
> *21-22).*

The gospel scenes we hear around Christmas time at first
appear disordered and confused. First we hear about the birth
of our savior at Bethlehem, which seems right, but then we hear
about the marriage feast at Cana, about the transformation of
water into wine. Next we find ourselves present when the magi
come from the East to pay homage to the infant Jesus. And now
we are presented with the baptism of Jesus. Biographically,
these scenes do not belong together; they occur far from each
other in time and place. But the church is not especially concerned with the biography of our Lord, and the theme of Christmas time is not to report the historical development of God-
Man Jesus Christ.

The essential message is how God can appear in our human
world and how God is revealed in Jesus Christ. In order to
understand this mystery the evangelists use many representa-
tions, ones that have again and again been deeply felt and
believed in the different religions.

We understand how God can become visible in our lives when
we comprehend how God is revealed in what is small and apparently insignificant — like the divine child, born in a manger in
Bethlehem. If we dare to say yes to what is undeveloped and
small within ourselves by trusting in the grace and guidance of

God in our lives, then we have understood one of the forms of God's self-revelation.

The marriage feast at Cana presents a picture of the eucharist as it was celebrated in the great religion of the God of wine, Dionysus, hundreds of years before Christianity. Dionysus was a god who died and was reborn, a god who was present in the acts of eating and drinking. He was a sign that life continues beyond death. God is present in the gifts of life. And when we can experience life as holy in this way and ourselves as immortal, then our human will conforms to the will of God and we find that the transformation of water and wine at Cana signifies a holy marriage between God and humanity that takes place right here and now in our own lives.

When we understand that the power of God in our lives does not come from outside, that it does not happen by command or by force, but that it blazes up like a light in the darkness, a light that attracts us and guides us through the night, then we understand the miracle of the magi. When we find God in the outskirts of civilization, not in the courts and palaces but in the inconspicuous, and when we pay homage to that which appears so unimportant and small, then we understand what the story of the magi wants to tell us.

The scene of the baptism of Jesus on the Jordan is yet another image. According to the church, it closes the Christmas readings. And here also the heavens descend to touch the earth, while the human in Christ ascends to touch the firmament. The two meet each other face to face in this world. On the one side is John the Baptist, the greatest that humanity has brought forth; on the other side is the greatest truth of God, the calling of the Son.

John told everyone who thought he might be the messiah that he only baptized with water. He represents the never-ending effort that men and women of all times have made to purify, wash, and cleanse themselves, to make themselves as immaculate as possible in an almost desperate attempt to bring their lives into order, to guide their actions according to what is proper and correct, to clarify their motives, and to perfect their personalities.

But despite all that we can achieve through this purifying and washing, despite all that we can change externally, nothing really begins to live in this way. We often hear people complain that their external lives are perfectly in order, the furniture, the tables, the walls, everything around them is just the way it should be. They do what they are supposed to do, they perform all their duties. Day after day they carry out the tasks assigned to them. They are not aware of having made any mistakes, but still they feel a quietly growing despair, for nothing seems to live. There is nothing that sustains them, nothing that comes from within to open them up and give their lives form and meaning. What is life all about? Why do I do all the things I do? What does it all mean? These questions disturb their peace.

We need another initiation into life, another kind of baptism in order to find ourselves and to discover God. But it is nothing we can make happen ourselves; there is no way to get to it "from beneath." This is the limit of John's proclamation, and he knows this very well, so much so that he speaks of his preaching and mission as though it were the work of a mere slave, as though he himself were insignificant and powerless. After me, he says, there will come someone who *really* has power and strength. He will baptize you with the spirit and with fire.

This is the idea of a life that is worth living. No one knows exactly what happens, but each one of us who has experienced it knows what it feels like and can never forget it or turn away from it. We try to explain it in metaphors. We say that a spark has ignited in our lives. We say that we feel suddenly inspired, that we have been touched by something, that we are sustained by a goal and an idea, that we are possessed by a passion. All at once, we—who before were freezing in our well-heated houses and apartments—feel a warmth and an illumination within us. We know that we have now truly begun to live our lives. We are full of light and of love.

The scene in which this happens is described by the gospel in two images that are best understood in terms of the ancient Egyptian religion. The heavens open up and the spirit of God descends visibly in the form of a dove. The ancient Egyptians would see this as the opposite of the picture of death. They thought that when a person died, the soul flew up to heaven like a dove carrying the spark of light from the human heart back to the stars, so that the human spirit could melt together with the immutable light of the heavens and become one with the glory of the divine sun. The image of the descending dove says the opposite. It tell us that God gives us a true life beyond death, that God comes to meet and to receive the movement of our hearts, a movement that carries us upon the wings of longing. God does not wait for us to die, but the heavens open up and the spirit descends upon us here and now.

To see the heavens open up before us means suddenly to look at and be able to touch that which we have dreamed about all our life—almost without daring to hope that it was real. It means to grasp with our hands and be certain of what we expected, but were almost resigned to not receiving. It means to experience the surprise of being given what we felt was the best we had in us, a quality we never really knew how to realize because of fear and because it was buried over with worries and cares. The meaning of our lives, our true nature, which so often was covered over with clouds and caught in the downpour of sadness, which we were aware of only in glimpses and in despair, suddenly descends upon us like a ray of light from above. This is the beginning of a kind of heaven upon earth and of a great happiness.

And so we really believe that it is a voice from heaven itself, it says: "You are my beloved son, today I have chosen you." These words also come from Egypt. The son of the pharaoh was born as the child of a mortal father and mother, but when he ascended the throne, the god of heaven spoke these same words: "You are my beloved son, my chosen one." The ancient Egyptians were saying that we don't understand the divine king, the pharaoh, when we think of him as the child of human parents. Nor do we understand the mystery of the divine king when we say he was born of human will and the instincts of the flesh. We understand him and his true life only when we see it with the eyes of God, only when we see it as something that happens by means of God's recognition alone, for God wants this man to be divine.

We will feel the baptism that Jesus gives us in spirit and fire only to the extent that we see the royal dignity of our own lives like a light rising in us, when we feel in ourselves what the

Egyptian religion believed possible only for the pharaoh. We are called to be children of God. Every single human life is chosen by God to be given heavenly glory, eternal worth, and infinite respect and greatness. We are allowed to think of ourselves with pride and to accept our lives with enthusiasm. We no longer have to worry about purifying what is dirty and unclean; rather, we can live full of joy about the value and dignity we possess.

Then we will finally know how God can enter into our lives. Then we will also understand how what is small and inconspicuous in Bethlehem can be so great, how Jesus can be adulated with joy in Nazareth, how the whole of life—eating, drinking, everything from birth to death and resurrection—can be one single transformation of the earthly into the divine.

And in all this we will have understood the divine within our own lives and the inexhaustible grace of God. The heavens are open for us, and this means to believe in Jesus Christ and in the baptism he gives us.